Jobs and the
Labor Force of Tomorrow

THE URBAN AGENDA

Series Editor, Michael A. Pagano

A list of books in the series appears at the end of this book.

Jobs and the Labor Force of Tomorrow

Migration, Training, Education

EDITED BY MICHAEL A. PAGANO

University of Illinois at Chicago

PUBLISHED FOR THE
COLLEGE OF URBAN PLANNING
AND PUBLIC AFFAIRS (CUPPA),
UNIVERSITY OF ILLINOIS AT CHICAGO,
BY THE UNIVERSITY OF ILLINOIS PRESS
Urbana, Chicago, and Springfield

The College of Urban Planning and Public Affairs of the University of Illinois at Chicago and the University of Illinois Press gratefully acknowledge that publication of this book was assisted by a grant from the John D. and Catherine T. MacArthur Foundation.

Library of Congress Control Number: 2017949936
978-0-252-04153-2 (hardcover)
978-0-252-08314-3 (paperback)
978-0-252-05015-2 (e-book)

Contents

Preface and Acknowledgments

The year of the 2016 presidential election engaged the nation in an animated conversation about jobs, immigration, and trade, or in the lexicon of academia, "human capital." Dynamic metropolitan economies require a diverse, trained, and available workforce that adapts to the needs of commerce, industry, government, and the service sector today as well as in the future. The rapidly changing economy demands that the workforce be adaptable and flexible by continuously increasingly skill levels, providing training opportunities, and recognizing the quick pace of job shifting. The quality of the workforce and supply of human capital in U.S. urban areas have been shaped by a variety of forces throughout the industrial and postindustrial eras, most notably the enactment of compulsory public education, inducement of internal migration, massive demands for a rapidly increasing workforce via immigration, and the enactment of public-policy regulations concerning wages, working conditions, and collective bargaining. The 2016 Urban Forum focused its lens on human capital development to address the contemporary challenges that shape human capital in metropolitan regions by examining the role of migration and immigration, K–12 education preparedness, postsecondary workforce training and development efforts, and recruitment and professional development of Millennials.

The 2016 event was cochaired by Cook County Board president Toni Preckwinkle; Juan Salgado, who is president of the Instituto del Progreso Latino; and UIC Chancellor Michael Amiridis. The event was held on September 15, attracting five hundred students, community activists, private citizens, government and nonprofit leaders, and many others. The keynote address was presented by award-winning columnist Clarence Page. A senior member of the Chicago Tribune editorial board and a regular panelist on *The McLaughlin Group*, Page also serves as a guest panelist on CBS's *Face the Nation*. He is a regular contributor of essays to *PBS News Hour*, has hosted documentaries on the Public Broadcasting System, and is the 1989 Pulitzer Prize winner for Commentary.

The 2016 UIC Urban Forum's external board of advisors includes the following:

- Clarence Anthony, executive director, National League of Cities
- MarySue Barrett, president, Metropolitan Planning Council
- Henry Cisneros, former secretary, HUD; former mayor, San Antonio; founder and chairman, CityView
- Rahm Emanuel, mayor, Chicago
- Lee Fisher, president and CEO, CEOs for Cities
- Karen Freeman-Wilson, mayor, Gary
- Bruce Katz, Centennial Scholar, Brookings Institution
- Jeff Malehorn, president and CEO, World Business Chicago
- Terry Mazany, president and CEO, Chicago Community Trust
- Toni Preckwinkle, president, Cook County Board
- Julia Stasch, president, John D. and Catherine T. MacArthur Foundation
- Joseph Szabo, executive director, Chicago Metropolitan Agency for Planning
- Susana Vasquez, vice president for Strategic Initiatives and Resource Development, Illinois Facilities Fund

Three panels were formed to discuss the broad range of human capital issues. The first was titled "Evolving Pathways to Work," and sitting on the panel were

- James Heckman, Nobel Prize economist, professor, University of Chicago
- Theresa E. Mintle, president and CEO, Chicagoland Chamber of Commerce
- Juan Salgado, president and CEO, Instituto del Progreso Latino

John McCarron, columnist and former editorial board member of the *Chicago Tribune*, moderated the panel.

The second panel, "The Jobless Economy," included

- George Crabtree, director, UIC Energy Initiative; Distinguished Professor of Physics, UIC; director of the Joint Center for Energy Storage (JCESR) at Argonne National Laboratory
- Beth Swanson, vice president of Strategy and Programs, Joyce Foundation

- Julie Friedman Steele, founder and CEO, 3D Printer Experience; board of directors and interim executive director, World Future Society

The panel was moderated by Sarah Karp, reporter, WBEZ.

The last panel of the day focused on issues of immigration and migration. The panelists on "Bridges or Walls? Immigration and Trade Policy" included

- Oscar Chacón, cofounder and executive director, Alianza Americas
- Pin Ni, president, Wanxiang America
- Héctor R. Cordero-Guzmán, professor, School of Public and International Affairs, Baruch College, City University of New York

Chip Mitchell, West Side Bureau reporter, WBEZ, moderated the panel.

A concluding keynote address on the "inclusive economy" was presented by Terry Mazany, president and CEO of the Chicago Community Trust.

The presidential election and the continuing controversy and conversation surrounding jobs, immigration, the jobless economy, international trade and the like, demonstrated the critical importance of discussing these "human capital" issues in a public, open, and interactive setting. An undertaking of this magnitude requires an investment of time and resources on the part of an outstanding group of dedicated employees who invested untold hours in planning, designing, and managing the event. In particular, I am indebted to the outstanding conference management skills of Jenny Sweeney and Elle Ullum, who orchestrated the event with the generous support of Jasculca-Terman Associates, especially Karla Bailey. Other UIC personnel who were active and supportive of the various tasks and activities of the process include Jennifer Woodard, Darcy Evon, Norma Ramos, and Bill Burton. The graduate assistants who worked on this project were Rudy Faust and Jantel Hines. I am deeply grateful to the entire team for their superb job in creating the event and for their indomitable spirit of working together for another successful event.

The editorial assistance and manuscript supervision by Rudy Faust, who was responsible for writing the summary of the panelists' conversations (part 3 of this book, which synthesizes panelists' salient comments) and who was responsible for the book production process, is owed a deep debt of gratitude.

The annual UIC Urban Forum offers thought-provoking, engaged, and insightful conferences on critical urban issues in a venue to which all of the world's citizens are invited.

Michael A. Pagano
Director of the UIC Urban Forum and Dean, College of Urban Planning and Public Affairs, University of Illinois at Chicago
January 2017

PART ONE
OVERVIEW

The Future of Work

Urban Economies in Transition

BETH GUTELIUS AND NIK THEODORE

URBAN ECONOMIES AFTER THE GREAT RECESSION

Major metropolitan areas have long been the principal sites of economic change in the United States. Home to 80 percent of the population and responsible for 84 percent of gross domestic product, large metropolitan areas (those with more than 150,000 inhabitants) are the drivers of the nation's vibrant and diverse economy.[1] This, however, is only part of the story. Industrial restructuring has gutted the jobs base of many localities, while others have experienced robust growth. Many workers have seen their conditions of employment eroded by transformations in workforce systems and the deterioration of labor standards. As a result, many of the nation's inequalities are most starkly visible in urban economies.

Concerns over job security and downward economic mobility are widespread across the United States.[2] Economic anxieties have exacerbated social conflicts within cities, and these tensions are being expressed through electoral politics as well as popular protest. After decades of being relegated to the "back burner" of policy debates, the problems of economic inequality and regional uneven development have become central issues in political campaigns at all levels of government. The 2016 presidential campaign, for example, was strongly shaped by economic populism by both the left and the right as a diverse set of economic concerns, from international trade to the problems facing "inner cities" to financial regulation to immigration reform, were linked to the perennial election topics of taxation and job creation. At state and local levels, voters considered ballot initiatives that would increase the minimum wage, expand provision of paid sick leave, institute "right-to-work" laws designed to shrink unionization, and levy tax increases on the wealthy. These initiatives signal the increasing importance of states and localities in shaping the economic policy landscape.

To a large extent, the economic anxieties expressed by many Americans can be traced to changes that are underway in the nature of work, changes that have resulted in job instability and falling real incomes for many households. An increasing sense of labor market precariousness—the belief that one's place in the economy is not only uncertain but also being actively undermined by the largely invisible forces of trade and technology as well as by the capricious decisions of corporate managers—is reinforced by the often abrupt dislocations that are occurring within employers' workforce systems. Whether through outsourcing, temping, mass layoffs, or the pay raises and promotions that never come, an increasing share of the workforce is regularly reminded that job security isn't what it used to be.

Workforce quality is not simply a question of human capital acquisition through education, training, and job experience. Decisions on the demand side of the job market (those made by employers as they restructure workforce systems) can have significant impacts on supply-side conditions (worker availability and qualifications). Changes in job quality or labor demand can have important feedback effects on job seekers' decisions to invest in education and training. Workers may forego expenditures on training, for example, if they believe routes to advancement are closed or if they find that their job prospects are poor. Likewise, they may discontinue job searches if they believe such efforts are futile due to high unemployment levels. This chapter highlights some of the key characteristics of the U.S. workforce as well as some of the impacts recent economic changes have had on key labor market indicators. First we review recent changes in the composition and qualifications of the labor force. We then assess changes that are underway in the organization of work—in particular, the rise of the so-called "gig economy." The final section highlights some of the policy and enforcement initiatives that have been pursued by local governments and advocates in light of these changes.

EMPLOYMENT, WAGES, PRODUCTIVITY, AND INEQUALITY

Economic inequality has increased sharply over the past several decades, and is reflected in the divergence observed in multiple measures of financial well-being.[3] Two leading drivers of income inequality are the spread of low-wage work and the existence of widespread violations of labor standards, such as laws that are meant to guarantee minimum wages and overtime pay.[4] The deterioration of labor market conditions for workers during this "Age of Inequality," as Steven Pitts has termed it, can be partly attributed to the decoupling of the historic link between labor productivity and wages.[5] From the end of World War II until the early 1970s, productivity and wage increases virtually went hand in hand. In contrast, between 1973 and 2013, although worker productivity rose by 74.4 percent, hourly compensation increased by just 9.2 percent.[6] The results have been widening inequality, the spread of low-wage jobs, and mounting family economic hardship. Simply put, prosperity is not being shared.

The Great Recession and the jobless recovery that followed exacerbated many of the difficulties facing workers. Not only did the post–Great Recession economic recovery fail to generate a sufficient number of jobs to absorb the unemployed and new labor market entrants, but the pattern of job losses and gains across the business cycle was skewed in favor of jobs in low-wage industries.[7] The economic downturn disproportionately removed higher-wage jobs from the economy while the recovery added a disproportionate number of jobs in lower-wage industries (fig. 1).[8] In the competitive postrecession labor market many jobseekers had few options but to settle for positions at pay rates well below those of their previous jobs.

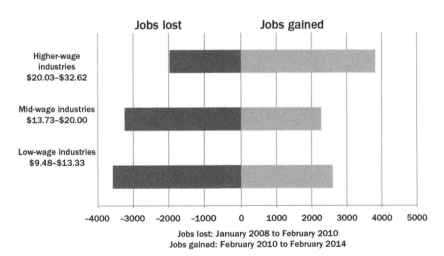

Figure 1. Net Change in Private Sector Employment (in thousands)
Source: Annette Bernhardt, *The Low-Wage Recovery: Industry Employment and Wages Four Years into the Recovery* (New York: National Employment Law Project, 2014).

The Great Recession, like the two previous recessions, seems to have signaled a second worrying change in patterns of job growth during economic recoveries. Historically, unemployment rates dropped quickly at the end of a recession as hiring resumed at a brisk pace (fig. 2). Beginning with the 1990s recovery, however, slow growth became the norm and unemployment rates remained persistently high. Since the early 1990s, the economic recoveries have been "jobless recoveries," periods of macroeconomic growth that are not accompanied by commensurate levels of job growth. Jobless recoveries are damaging to the employment and earnings of all unemployed workers, but certain demographic groups are particularly hard hit by slower than expected job growth.

Over the past thirty years, the African American unemployment rate has been double that of whites, while the rate for Latinos tends to fall somewhere between those of blacks and whites.[9] Moreover, researchers at the Economic Policy Institute report that "during recessions the black-white gap in unemployment rates increases, as the unemployment rate of blacks increases more than that of whites. The same is true for the unemployment gap between Hispanic and white workers, though to a lesser extent. Between 2007 and 2010, the unemployment rate of whites increased by 4.2 percentage points (from 3.9 percent to 8.0 percent), while that of blacks increased by 7.7

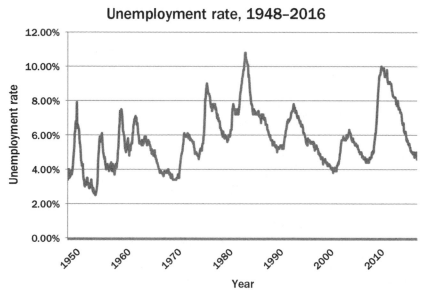

Figure 2. Unemployment Rate, 1948–2016
Source: U.S. Bureau of Labor Statistics, *Current Population Survey*, 2016.

percentage points (from 8.3 percent to 15.9 percent) and that of Hispanics increased by 6.8 percentage points (from 5.6 percent to 12.5 percent)."[10] The impacts of these patterns of job loss have been devastating for the wealth accumulation levels of African American and Latino households. As the U.S. economy slipped into recession, African American and Latino families were poorly positioned to sustain income losses, in large part because of their low levels of wealth accumulation. And then the bottom fell out of the economy. Between 2007 and 2010, African American families experienced a 31 percent decline in wealth, while Latino families experienced a staggering 40 percent decline in wealth.[11] Though declines in wealth accumulation were experienced by all three races or ethnicities, by 2010, whites had, on average, eight times more wealth than African Americas and nearly nine times more than Latinos. This unequal distribution of wealth became even greater during the first few years of the economic recovery. By 2013, the median wealth of white households was thirteen times that of black households and ten times that of Latino households.[12]

In part as a result of the trends outlined above, living standards among U.S. households are diverging. The Pew Research Center reports that "the share of U.S. adults living in middle income households fell to 50% in 2015, after more than four decades in which those households served as the nation's economic majority." Furthermore, according to Pew, "the financial gaps between middle- and upper-income Americans have widened, with upper-income households holding 49% of U.S. aggregate household income (up from 29% in 1970) and seven times as much wealth as middle-income households (up from three times as much in 1983)."[13]

Recent labor market entrants also are harmed by recessions and jobless recoveries. College graduates who enter the job market during recessions experience significant and persistent negative effects on their job opportunities over the course of their working lives, and young workers who enter the labor market during a jobless recovery often experience unemployment and are more likely to accept lower-skilled jobs and lower wages due to limited job openings available to them.[14] The impacts of entering the labor market during times of slow or negative job growth are enduring; fifteen years after graduation, the wages and career progression of these workers remain lower than those of workers who entered the labor market under stronger macroeconomic conditions.[15]

Long-run trends in labor force participation offer another indicator of the health of the U.S. labor market. The seasonally adjusted labor force participation rate in the U.S. rose fairly steadily from 58.6 percent in January 1965 to

66.8 percent in January 1990.[16] It fluctuated slightly between 1990 and 2001 before beginning its decline in the 2001 recession and falling more sharply following the 2007–9 Great Recession. In September 2015, labor force participation dipped to 62.4 percent, a level that had not been seen since 1977. The labor force participation rate of men has been in decline for nearly sixty years. For decades, this decline was offset by substantial increases in women's labor force participation, particularly from the 1950s through the 1980s before slowing in the 1990–91 recession. Women's labor force participation rate rose from 33.4 percent in January 1950, to 38.4 percent in January 1965, and reaching 57.8 percent in November 1989.[17] Participation rates increased again during the economic recovery, peaking at 60.3 percent in April 2000. However, since that time, women's labor force participation has been in decline, falling to 56.5 in September 2015 (per the most recent available data). Falling labor force participation rates could be a sign of worker discouragement—jobseekers who have stopped looking for work due to weakness in the job market. An analysis of the factors that contributed to the decline in the labor force participation rate since the end of the Great Recession found that two-thirds of the decline is attributable to cyclical factors, while just one-third is caused by demographic factors, such as workers aging out of the labor market.[18]

Approximately one in six workers in the civilian labor force is foreign born, up from fewer than one in twenty in 1970.[19] This increase in the proportion of foreign-born workers in the U.S. labor market has been driven by immigration from Mexico and Central America.[20] This is significant because the average education level of these workers is lower than that of other foreign-born workers as well as the native-born workforce.[21] As a result, immigrants from Mexico and Central America are clustered in jobs requiring low levels of educational attainment.

Analysis by the Pew Research Center of changing job requirements in the U.S. economy finds that the job categories with the highest growth are those that require higher levels of education, technical competencies, and analytical skills.[22] As a result, workers at most levels of the occupational distribution will need to plan on participating in training programs over the course of their working lives if they are to be well positioned to succeed in the changing economy. While there is general consensus that workers will need to adopt an approach to continuous skills upgrading over the long term, there is less agreement on whether a skills mismatch is responsible for current levels of unemployment and underemployment.[23] Peter Cappelli argues that this is not due to a lack of skills in the labor market, noting that employer expectations have risen when it comes to hiring new workers.[24] Rising expectations are attributable to a growing reluctance on the part of employers to invest in skills training. This has long-run consequences for skills development in the United States because public systems for apprenticeships and training are limited and underfunded.

THE COMING GIG ECONOMY?

Perhaps no change in employment relationships has been more heralded—and more confusing—than that associated with the "gig economy." According to economists at the U.S. Bureau of Labor Statistics, "a gig describes a single project or task for which a worker is hired, often through a digital marketplace, to work on demand."[25] Gigs are short-term assignments, often project-based, that are accepted on an as-needed basis by independent workers. Gig workers may be employed simultaneously by multiple employers, or they may have a single client at any point in time. The common attribute of jobs in the gig economy is that they differ from the traditional model of a full-time position, with implicit employment stability, with a single employer. This has important implications for career ladders and pathways since mobility for gig economy workers principally occurs across employers and industries rather than within them, as it had for many workers in decades past. It also can have impacts on income levels over the course of a career since on-demand work tends to be plentiful when the economy is strongest and harder to acquire during economic downturns, and on annual incomes since time off of work between projects or tasks results in an immediate loss of earnings.

Ways of finding work also are changing, and the growth of the gig economy is often attributed to the development of online labor platforms that enable the creation of smooth-functioning markets for temporary work assignments. Digital platforms such as Uber, FlexJobs, TaskRabbit, and Handy connect employers with prospective gig workers for jobs as varied as software developer, tax accountant, electrician, home cleaner, and driver. Gig work is often touted for its flexibility. It may allow workers greater freedom to tailor their schedules than what is allowed under traditional employment arrangements. Gig workers are their own bosses, so to speak, and the autonomy that short-term, task-based work affords can be highly valued. But there are significant downsides as well. Employment opportunities may be sporadic and uncertain, leaving workers with prolonged periods of inactivity—and no pay. In addition, gig work does not include employer-provided health care benefits or unemployment insurance, nor does it include sick leave or vacation time.

Gig workers may also have difficulty accessing credit because lenders may be wary about the inconsistency of project-based work.

The gig economy includes workers who are hired under a disparate set of employment arrangements, such as contingent workers who do not have a contract for long-term employment; independent contractors, freelancers, and independent consultants; and various types of on-call arrangements. The variability of these employment relationships has resulted in widely varying estimates of the size of the gig workforce. Government statistics on this segment of the labor force were most recently collected in 2005, and the categories that were used to collect employment figures do not provide much insight into the changes that are underway.[26] To fill the data gap, researchers, private firms, and workers' organizations have stepped in to undertake studies that estimate the size of the contingently employed workforce. Taken together, these studies result in a perplexing picture of the "new economy" and its workforce, though each provides some insights into the conditions that have led to an increase in nonstandard employment.

A survey by the Freelancers Union and the digital platform Upwork estimated that in 2016 fully 35 percent of the U.S. workforce "engaged in supplemental, temporary, contract- or project-based work, within the past 12 months."[27] A considerable majority of survey respondents (79%) reported that they prefer freelancing to traditional employment, with many citing greater autonomy and better work-life balance as key to their job satisfaction. McKinsey Global Institute (MGI) estimates that approximately 27 percent of the working-age population in the U.S. is involved in a form of independent earning outside of a traditional employment arrangement.[28] More than half of these workers use gigs to supplement incomes earned through other means, and almost one-third would prefer a traditional job if an appropriate one would be found. McKinsey Global Institute researchers find that the gig economy includes substantial numbers of youths as well as seniors, men as well as women, and members of low-income households. One-third of gig workers are classified by MGI as "free agents" who willingly pursue this form of employment and derive their primary income from independent work. Another 40 percent are "casual earners" who use independent work to supplement their regular incomes. Among those who find few options outside of independent work, 14 percent are "reluctant" gig workers who would prefer traditional employment and another 14 percent are "financially strapped" and engage in gig work to supplement their income but would prefer not to have to do so.

In contrast to those studies that report an explosive increase in alternative employment arrangements, other research suggests that these changes, though still significant, are not quite as dramatic. In her review of the growth of various forms of contingent work, Annette Bernhardt concludes that despite the "strong intuition that the nature of work has fundamentally changed ... it has been hard to find evidence of a strong, unambiguous shift toward nonstandard or contingent forms of work."[29] Bernhardt cautions that while there has been growth in alternative and independent work arrangements, traditional employment arrangements remain the norm and likely will be so for the foreseeable future. But perhaps now there are signs of unambiguous change. Analyzing survey questions included in the Rand American Life Panel, Lawrence F. Katz and Alan B. Krueger found that the percentage of workers engaged in alternative work arrangements—workers employed through temporary help agencies, on-call workers, contract workers, and independent contractors or freelancers—increased from 10.1 percent in early 2005 to 15.8 percent in late 2015.[30] While the figure of approximately 16 percent of the workforce employed in contingent work relationships is not as eye-popping as estimates reported in many other studies, the growth in nonstandard employment is noteworthy. The incidence of employment in nonstandard jobs was found to be greater among older workers as well as those who earn higher wages. In terms of industry composition, professional and business services, health and education, and other services industries accounted for half of all of workers employed in an alternative work arrangement. Despite finding that a smaller share of U.S. workers are employed in nonstandard employment arrangements than some of the other surveys that have been conducted, Katz and Krueger still arrive at a startling conclusion: "*all of the net employment growth in the U.S. economy from 2005 to 2015 appears to have occurred in alternative work arrangements*" (original emphasis).[31] This suggests that during the recovery following the Great Recession, the terms of employment of many newly created jobs are based on the principles of contingent work in the on-demand economy: flexibility and employment with few guarantees.

Online gig work, often mediated by a digital platform, has come to symbolize the tensions of the changing nature of work. Yet for all the debate produced by this small segment of the economy, the best evidence we have to date estimates that on-demand employment comprises, at most, 1 percent of the U.S. workforce.[32] The JP Morgan Chase Institute analyzed data from its bank clients and offered an illuminating look at worker participation on online platforms, finding that those participating in the on-demand economy do so primarily as a stopgap measure to mitigate income volatility—in other words, when incomes dip in primary jobs, workers seek secondary, short-term gig work to make up the difference. While the number of people participating on labor platforms like Uber and Handy is growing, workers' reliance on income from platforms has not changed—they are not picking up more hours in total, and overall earnings have not increased. Most workers who are active on online platforms are earning less than a quarter of their income from these digital markets, and there is little evidence that workers are moving wholesale from other work to platform-mediated work in the gig economy.

These data raise important questions about the root causes of income in-stability within the sectors in which on-demand workers have their primary job. Labor platforms are beginning to establish themselves as new interme-diaries in processes of labor market adjustment, and wage stagnation and macroeconomic volatility provide the unique set of circumstances in which supplemental income is necessary. Even while the on-demand economy may not (yet) be drawing a substantial portion of workers away from the tradi-tional job market, it is clearly shaping a secondary labor market, allowing for important opportunities for workers to smooth incomes from month to month when work hours in their primary jobs fluctuate.

Although the extent to which the gig economy has grown remains a matter of some dispute, it does appear clear that this growth has primarily occurred in major cities. An analysis by the Brookings Institution of changes in the number of non-employer firms—those that earned revenues but employed no workers, usually self-employed, unincorporated sole proprietors—finds that much of the increase in the gig economy is attributable to the "rides and rooms" sectors of major cities.[33] In other words, so-called ride-sharing ser-vices such as Uber, Lyft, and Via as well as room-sharing services like Airbnb, FlipKey, and HomeAway account for much of the growth in non-employer firms that occurred between 2010 and 2014. Leaving aside the observation that labeling these services as being part of a "sharing economy" is a misno-mer given that these companies are profit-making ventures through which services are sold not shared, the data show that major metropolitan areas are home to much of the observed growth. This should not be surprising, since major metropolitan areas historically have been engines of economic growth as well as key sites for economic change and industrial restructuring.

The precise distributional consequences of gigging and other forms of independent working are not known, though if the number of workers hired into nonstandard employment arrangements continues to increase, it is likely that these job market changes will have impacts on patterns of socioeco-nomic inequality. By all accounts, the rise of the gig economy has occurred in conjunction with a slowly recovering national economy, one that struggled to regain its momentum following the Great Recession. Faced with an inhospitable job market, some workers turned to nonstandard employment as their route back into work. Others sought to supplement their incomes through on-call assignments in an effort to make ends meet. As the recovery gathered pace, many of the new jobs created saw the terms and conditions of employment radically altered. What remains to be seen is how this sector changes when the economy slows. With little in the way of job security, independently employed workers are vulnerable to hiring cutbacks and spending freezes by companies and decreases in consumer spending by employer households. Gig economy workers may find themselves chasing fewer and fewer opportunities at a time when recently unemployed workers quickly join their ranks. The increased competition for work during lean periods would likely drive down compensation levels while also leaving many job seekers out of work. Without an effective social safety net in place to cushion the blow of an economic downturn on earnings from the on-demand economy, workers are exposed to heightened risks and hardships that, if not planned for, would be detrimental to their well-being.

Threats to incomes from decreases in employment opportunities are not the only problems facing participants in the gig economy. Research has found evidence of widespread racial discrimination against both workers and customers, with African Americans bearing the brunt of discriminatory practices.[34] In late 2016, the U.S. Equal Employment Opportunity Commission stated in its strategic enforcement plan for 2017–21 that it plans to look into whether companies in the gig economy are misclassifying employees as independent contractors in an effort to evade their obligations under federal employment bias laws.[35] The implications of gigging on labor standards could be far-reaching. It is possible that, workplace discrimination cases aside, workers increasingly will be misclassified as independent contractors as employers look to shed many of the legal liabilities (e.g., meeting unemployment insurance requirements and abiding by overtime laws) associated with the traditional employment model and do so under the guise of evolving gig economy protocols.[36] Independent contractor misclassification poses serious problems, not just for workers who experience a loss of workplace protections and employment benefits, but also for governments that lose tax revenues while also seeing unemployment insurance and workers' compensation insurance programs strained under new fiscal burdens. For these reasons, it is not surprising that the gig economy has been the target of class-action lawsuits and other litigation. With governments being slow to redefine regulations so that they cover on-demand workers, it may be the courts that have a greater say in determining the contours of—and conditions within—the growing gig economy.

The gig economy has garnered much attention in part because of its novel uses of technology to mediate employment relationships. Labor and capital platforms have been heralded as new phenomena, ones that reveal the inadequacies of existing labor laws because the latter are said to interfere with innovation. Platforms are just one way that technology is changing the organization of work. Scheduling software has gained prominence as a key tool in firms' labor flexibility strategies, especially in scheduling variable shifts for retail workers. The proven efficiency of such tools for "scheduling to demand," however, is at odds with workers' needs for stability, and it therefore impacts family life and well-being.[37]

Similar to the hype surrounding the gig economy is the prediction that the coming age of robots and automation will upend employment in many sectors, from health care to manufacturing to finance, and portend widespread technologically induced unemployment. In one prominent analysis, Carl Benedikt Frey and Michael A. Osborne examined hundreds of occupations and categorized them as facing high, medium, or low levels of risk for computerization.[38] The authors estimate that, over the next twenty years, 47 percent of total U.S. employment is at high risk for computer automation. Additionally, the authors found that the higher the wages and educational attainment associated with an occupation, the more likely it is to be affected by technology. Futurists like Eric Brynjolfsson and Andrew McAfee agree, arguing that the long-run prospects for many workers, especially lower-skilled workers, is bleak.[39]

The Organization for Economic Cooperation and Development has taken a more nuanced approach to assessing the implications of automation for job losses, breaking down jobs into their constituent activities. This task-based approach results in a significantly lower estimate of automatable jobs, at just 9 percent of jobs in the U.S.[40] Echoing this line of inquiry, other observers argue that technology has been, and will continue to complement—not substitute—human labor. As a result, automation will transform jobs but not necessarily replace human with digital or robotic labor. The effects of technological advancement, though, will be uneven: low-skill workers, whose jobs are more susceptible to automation, will bear the brunt of this change and thus require attention from policy makers to mitigate the negative impacts on their livelihoods. This points to the need for policy and labor standards that are sensitive to changes in the organization of work and to the needs of workers themselves, and in many cases this is happening at the municipal level.

LABOR STANDARDS AND MUNICIPAL POLICY

Once primarily confined to the domain of federal policy making, the agenda for raising the floor on wages and working conditions, particularly in low-wage industries, is now actively being pursued in cities. Advocates for workers' rights have capitalized on the long-run trend toward devolving power to state and local levels in order to advance a range of pro-worker policies. This has proven especially important in light of congressional inaction in minimum wage policy, as well as in updating the system of workplace protections so they keep pace with a rapidly changing economy. Emerging strategies to improve workers' rights that are based in urban policy making rely on an ecosystem of progressive organizations, cross-sector coalitions, labor unions, worker centers, immigrant rights advocates, and community groups. This ecosystem increasingly is shaping the political context in which struggles over local employment policy occur. Below are examples of some of the forms municipal experimentation has taken to address employment practices that harm segments of the U.S. labor force.[41]

Increasing the minimum wage. In response to lack of action at the federal level to raise the minimum wage—which is $7.25 and was last increased in 2007—thirty cities, twenty-six states, and the District of Columbia have asked voters to approve wages higher than the federal minimum.[42] Some cities and states have also eliminated the tipped minimum wage, which stands at $2.13 nationally, and instituted a single wage applicable to all industries. In order to address stagnation over time due to increases in the cost of living, the higher minimum wage in some places is indexed to inflation.

Providing paid leave and sick time. Family and medical leave policies in the United States are woefully inadequate—the United States is the only industrialized nation that does not offer paid parental leave, though workers can take unpaid leave under the Family Medical Leave Act. Twenty-nine cities have passed paid leave provisions that establish minimum requirements for the amount of paid leave workers can earn, the conditions under which they can use the time, and amount of pay they receive.[43]

Penalizing wage theft. Anti–wage theft ordinances at state and local levels are now in effect in dozens of cities and counties.[44] These laws are wide-ranging, including legislation that enables cities to refuse to award contracts to companies that have failed to properly pay their employees, calls for criminal penalties for wage theft, revokes the business license of any company found liable for wage violations, and broadens the laws under which workers can bring wage theft claims. Recent research suggests that state and local penalties for violating wage laws act to deter wage theft.[45]

Promoting fair scheduling. In 2015, a Retail Workers Bill of Rights went into effect in San Francisco, focused on jobs at chain retailers and restaurants.[46] Its provisions require employers to offer first right of refusal for additional hours to part-time workers, provide advance notice of scheduling, and compensate employees for last-minute changes to their work schedules, among other things. Efforts to mitigate the negative impacts of erratic scheduling on workers are underway in other cities as well.

Facilitating worker organizing. The New York City Council introduced a bill that would allow fast-food workers to designate a nonprofit workers' organization of their choosing, and mandate employers to automatically deduct "dues" from workers' paychecks to contribute to the organization.[47] While not a labor union with legal collective bargaining rights, the effort would facilitate worker organizing and provide a mechanism for financial sustainability by connecting workers to organizations that advocate on their behalf to improve working conditions. In Seattle, the city council passed an ordinance that allows, for the first time, independent contractor drivers to join a driver representative organization through which they can negotiate with employers.[48] Under the National Labor Relations Act, independent contractors are not eligible to bargain collectively, and they are also excluded from other basic provisions including minimum wage and health and safety laws. This bill is aimed at supporting workers in transportation network companies like Uber, as well as for-hire taxi companies.

Improving enforcement of labor standards. In the face of underfunded public-sector enforcement functions, workers' rights organizations have entered into partnerships with government agencies to improve enforcement of health and safety regulations and employment protections. Worker centers and other civil-society organizations, often in collaboration with high-road employers, partner with government inspectors to identify employers that are engaged in illegal workplace practices.[49] Workers' organizations use their deep relationships with workers who are denied labor protections to collect detailed information on employer practices. This information is then used by government agencies to strategically target high-violation employers and industries.

Connecting workforce training and workers' rights. A fundamental problem facing workers is the lack of good jobs that pay family supporting wages. No amount of training and education, re-skilling or up-skilling can change this dynamic, which represents a dilemma for workforce development practitioners and workers' rights advocates alike. The workforce development field, largely responsible for maintaining the infrastructure for worker training, has begun to shift in response to conditions in low-wage labor markets. For example, the Aspen Institute's Workforce Strategies Initiative proposes a tandem set of activities: building ladders for workers to gain experience and training so they can advance to better-paying jobs, and raising the floor on working conditions to improve the jobs for which these workers are being prepared.[50]

Workers' rights organizations are also leveraging innovations in technology to support their work—creating apps to record and report wage theft, or establishing new platforms that aggregate workers, facilitate the identification of the issues they face, and encourage them to take action. For example, the National Day Laborer Organizing Network, the New Immigrant Community Empowerment (a New York–based worker center), and the International Union of Painters and Allied Trades teamed up to create the first "wage theft app" that enables domestic workers and day laborers to use their smartphones to record the employment details that are vital to recovering unpaid wages in occupations with high rates of workplace violations.[51] In an effort to educate the employers of nannies and caregivers in private households, the National Domestic Workers Alliance has partnered with the online platform Care.com to promote the Fair Care Pledge and the Good Work Code, a set of guidelines for worker pay and conditions.[52] These early experiments attempt to harness technological innovations to meet the needs of workers in nonstandard employment arrangements while also enhancing workers' voices in the defense of labor standards.

The challenges workers face in contemporary labor markets are substantial, and changes in the organization of work, an outdated federal regulatory framework, and a restricted voice in the workplace have punitive effects on all workers, and especially those in low-wage industries. Cities are at once sites of vast inequalities and progressive innovation and experimentation, where local political will has proven to be a strong force in counteracting policy action and inaction that undermines workers' livelihoods and well-being. The operating theory of change is a bit of a long game: as local policies to support workers and their families become commonplace, covering the major population centers and economic hubs of the United States, this growing tide puts pressure on the federal government to act. In the meantime, urban policy making draws boundaries of reprieve, within which workers can access protection from some of the most harmful practices and trends underway in the economy today.

Notes

1. James Manyika, Jaana Remes, Richard Dobbs, Javier Orellana, and Fabian Schaer, *Urban America: US Cities in the Global Economy* (N.p.: McKinsey Global Institute, 2012).

2. Marketplace, Anxiety Index, accessed December 15, 2016, www.marketplace.org.

3. Lawrence Mishel, Josh Bivens, Elise Gould, and Heidi Shierholz, *The State of Working America*, 12th ed. (Ithaca, NY: Cornell University Press, 2012).

4. Laura Dresser, "Human Capital in Context: Policies that Shape Urban U.S. Labor Markets," chapter in this book; Ben Henry and Allyson Fredericksen, *Low Wage Nation: Nearly Half of New Jobs Don't Pay Enough to Make Ends Meet* (Seattle, WA: Alliance for a Just Society, 2016); Annette Bernhardt et al., *Broken Laws, Unprotected Workers: Violations of Employment and Labor Laws in American Cities* (New York: National Employment Law Project, 2009).

5. Steven Pitts, "Low-Wage Work in the Black Community in the Age of Inequality," in Sean Thomas-Breitfeld, Linda Burnham, Steven Pitts, Marc Bayard, and Algernon Austin, *#BlackWorkersMatter* (Boston, MA: Discount Foundation and Neighborhood Funders Group, 2015).

6. Ibid., 30.

7. Mishel et al., *State of Working America*, chapter 5.

8. Annette Bernhardt, *The Low-Wage Recovery: Industry Employment and Wages Four Years into the Recovery* (New York: National Employment Law Project, 2014).

9. Mishel et al., *State of Working America*, 339–40.

10. Ibid., 339.

11. Signe-Mary McKernan, Caroline Ratcliffe, Eugene Steuerle, and Sisi Zhang, *Less than Equal: Racial Disparities in Wealth Accumulation* (Washington, DC: Urban Institute, 2013).

12. Rakesh Kochhar and Richard Fry, "Wealth Inequality Has Widened along Racial, Ethnic Lines since End of Great Recession," FactTank: News in the Numbers, Pew Research Center, December 12, 2014.

13. D'Vera Cohn and Andrea Caumont, "10 Demographic Trends that Are Shaping the U.S. and the World," FactTank: News in the Numbers, Pew Research Center, March 31, 2016, accessed December 7, 2016, www.pewresearch.org.

14. Lisa B. Kahn, "The Long-Term Labor Market Consequences of Graduating from College in a Bad Economy," *Labour Economics* 17, no. 2 (2010): 303–16.

15. Ibid.

16. Federal Reserve Bank of St. Louis, "Civilian Labor Force Participation Rate: Women," accessed December 1, 2016, https://fred.stlouisfed.org/series/LNS11300002.

17. Ibid.

18. Heidi Shierholz, Labor Force Participation: Cyclical versus Structural Changes since the Start of the Great Recession (Washington, DC: Economic Policy Institute, 2012).

19. Audrey Singer, *Immigrant Workers in the U.S. Labor Force* (Washington, DC: Brookings Institution, 2012).

20. Xóchitl Bada, "Immigration to the United States in the Post–Civil Rights Years," chapter in this book; Héctor Cordero-Guzmán and Desiree Nuñez, "Immigrant Labor and the U.S. Economy: A Profile," *New Labor Forum* 22, no. 2 (2013): 16–27.

21. Cordero-Guzmán and Nuñez, "Immigrant Labor and the U.S. Economy"; Congressional Budget Office, *The Role of Immigrants in the U.S. Labor Market: An Update* (Washington, D.C.: Congress of the United States, July 2010).

22. "The State of American Jobs: How the Shifting Economic Landscape in Reshaping Work and Society and Affecting the Way People Think about the Skills and Training They Need to Get Ahead," Social Trends, Pew Research Center, October 6, 2016.

23. R. Jason Faberman and Bhashkar Mazumder, "Is There a Skills Mismatch in the Labor Market?," *Chicago Fed Letter* 300 (2012).

24. Peter Cappelli, *Why Good People Can't Get Jobs: The Skills Gap and What Companies Can Do about It* (Philadelphia, PA: Wharton Digital Press, 2012).

25. Elka Torpey and Andrew Hogan, "Working in a Gig Economy," U.S. Bureau of Labor Statistics, May 2016, accessed December 15, 2016, www.bls.gov.

26. New government statistics will be available after the Census Bureau administers the Contingent Worker Supplement to the Current Population Survey in May 2017.

27. Freelancers Union and Upwork, "Freelancing in America: 2016," Freelancers Union and Upwork, 2016.

28. James Manyika, Susan Lund, Jacques Bughin, Kelsey Robinson, Jan Mischke, and Deepa Mahajan, "Independent Work: Choice, Necessity, and the Gig Economy," McKinsey Global Institute Report, October 2016.

29. Annette Bernhardt, *Labor Standards and the Reorganization of Work: Gaps in Data and Research*, IRLE Working Paper 100-14 (Berkeley, CA: Institute for Research on Labor and Employment, 2014).

30. Lawrence F. Katz and Alan B. Krueger, "The Rise and Nature of Alternative Work Arrangements in the United States, 1995–2015," unpublished paper, March 29, 2016, accessed December 8, 2016, https://krueger.princeton.edu/sites/default/files/akrueger/files/katz_krueger_cws_-_march_29_20165.pdf.

31. Ibid., 7.

32. Diana Farrell and Fiona Greig, "Paychecks, Paydays, and the Online Platform Economy: Big Data on Income Volatility," JPMorgan Chase Institute, February 2016, accessed December 2, 2016, www.jpmorganchase.com; Katz and Krueger, "Rise and Nature."

33. Ian Hathaway and Mark Muro, *Tracking the Gig Economy: New Numbers* (Washington, DC: Brookings Institution, 2016).

34. Yanbo Ge, Christopher R. Knittel, Don MacKenzie, and Stephen Zoepf, *Racial and Gender Discrimination in Transportation Network Companies*, NBER Working Paper No. 22776 (Washington, DC: National Bureau of Economic Research, 2016); Benjamin G. Edelman and Michael Luca, "Digital Discrimination: The Case of

Airbnb.com," Harvard Business School NOM Unit Working Paper No. 14-054, January 10, 2014, doi:10.2139/ssrn.2377353; Devin G. Pope and Justin R. Sydnor, "What's in a Picture? Evidence of Discrimination from Prosper.com," *Journal of Human Resources* 46, no. 1 (2011): 53–92.

35. U.S. Equal Employment Opportunity Commission, *Strategic Enforcement Plan, Fiscal Years 2017–2021* (Washington, DC: Equal Employment Opportunities Commission, 2016).

36. Françoise Carré, *(In)dependent Contractor Misclassification*, EPI Briefing Paper 403 (Washington, DC: Economic Policy Institute, 2015).

37. Susan Lambert, "Passing the Buck: Labor Flexibility Practices that Transfer Risk onto Hourly Workers," *Human Relations* 61 (2008): 1203–27; National Women's Law Center, *Set Up for Success: Why Fair Schedules Are Critical for Working Parents and Their Children's Well-Being* (Washington, DC: National Women's Law Center, 2016).

38. Carl Benedikt Frey and Michael A. Osborne, "The Future of Employment: How Susceptible Are Jobs to Computerisation?," Oxford Martin School Programme on the Impacts of Future Technology Working Paper, September 17, 2013, accessed December 14, 2016, www.oxfordmartin.ox.ac.uk.

39. Erik Brynjolfsson and Andrew McAfee, *The Race against the Machine* (Lexington, MA: Digital Frontier Press, 2011).

40. Melanie Arntz, Terry Gregory, and Ulrich Zierahn, "The Risk of Automation for Jobs in OECD Countries: A Comparative Analysis," *OECD Social, Employment and Migration Working Papers*, no. 189 (Paris: OECD Publishing, 2016), doi:10.1787/5jlz9h56dvq7-en.

41. Annette Bernhardt, *The Role of Labor Market Regulation in Rebuilding Economic Opportunity in the U.S.* (New York: Roosevelt Institute, 2014); Marc Doussard and Ahmad Gamal, "The Rise of Wage Theft Laws: Can Community–Labor Coalitions Win Victories in State Houses?," *Urban Affairs Review* 52, no. 5 (2015): 780–807. A range of legislative efforts to lower labor standards have also been initiated at the state level. See Gordon Lafer, *The Legislative Attack on American Wages and Labor Standards, 2011–2012*, EPI Briefing Paper 364 (Washington, DC: Economic Policy Institute, 2013).

42. Economic Policy Institute Minimum Wage Tracker, accessed December 15, 2016, www.epi.org/minimum-wage-tracker/.

43. "Paid Sick Time Legislative Successes," *A Better Balance*, accessed December 6, 2016, www.abetterbalance.org/resources/paid-sick-time-legislative-successes/.

44. National Employment Law Project, *Winning Wage Justice: An Advocate's Guide to State and City Policies to Fight Wage Theft* (New York: National Employment Law Project, 2011); "Current and Pending Wage Theft Legislation," WageTheft.org, 2015, accessed December 12, 2016, www.wagetheft.org/local-and-state-legislation.

45. Daniel Galvin, "Deterring 'Wage Theft': Alt-Labor, State Politics, and the Policy Determinants of Minimum Wage Compliance," Working Paper Series, WP-15-08 (Evanston, IL: Northwestern University Institute for Policy Research, 2016).

46. "Formula Retail Employee Rights Ordinances," Office of Labor Standards Enforcement, City and County of San Francisco, accessed December 15, 2016, http://sfgov.org/olse/formula-retail-employee-rights-ordinances.

47. Int. 1384-2016, New York City Council, accessed December 1, 2016, http://legistar.council.nyc.gov/LegislationDetail.aspx?ID=2900907&GUID=3671A5D8-2C46-4169-978A-F318543B40A4.

48. "Giving Drivers a Voice: Council Unanimously Adopts First-of-Its-Kind Legislation to Give Drivers a Voice on the Job," Seattle City Council, press release, December 14, 2015, accessed December 15, 2016, www.seattle.gov/council/issues/giving-drivers-a-voice.

49. Janice Fine and Jennifer Gordon, "Strengthening Labor Standards Enforcement through Partnerships with Workers' Organizations," *Politics & Society* 38, no. 4 (2010): 552–85; Linda Delp and Kevin Riley, "Worker Engagement in the Health and Safety Regulatory Arena under Changing Models of Worker Representation," *Labor Studies Journal* 40, no. 1 (2015): 54–83; Janice Fine, *Co-Production: Bringing Together the Unique Capabilities of Government and Society for Stronger Labor Standards Enforcement* (New York: LIFT Fund, 2015); Shannon Gleeson, *Precarious Claims: The Promise and Failure of Workplace Protections in the United States* (Berkeley: University of California Press, 2017).

50. Economic Opportunities Program, *Build Ladders and Raise the Floor: Workforce Strategies Supporting Mobility and Stability for Low-Income Workers* (Washington, DC: Aspen Institute, 2014); see also Alison Dickson, Sue Davenport, and Marsha Love, *Workers' Rights for Workforce Development: A Practical Guide For Instructors and Job Seekers—Illinois Edition* (Chicago: Labor Education Program, School of Labor and Employment Relations, University of Illinois at Urbana-Champaign, 2015).

51. Liz Robbins, "New Weapon in Day Laborers' Fight against Wage Theft: A Smartphone App," *New York Times*, March 1, 2016, accessed December 12, 2016, www.nytimes.com; Linda Burnham and Nik Theodore, *Home Economics: The Invisible and Unregulated World of Domestic Work* (New York: National Domestic Workers Alliance, 2012); Abel Valenzuela, Nik Theodore, Edwin Melendez, and Ana Luz Gonzalez, *On the Corner: Day labor in the United States* (Los Angeles: UCLA Center for the Study of Urban Poverty, 2006).

52. Sarah Kessler, "The Domestic Workers Alliance Creates New Framework for Improving Gig Economy Jobs," 3 Minute Read, *Fast Company*, October 6, 2015, accessed December 15, 2016, www.fastcompany.com; see Fair Care Labs at www.faircarelabs.org for more information on employment standards for domestic workers.

PART TWO

WHITE PAPERS

Human Capital in Context

Policies that Shape Urban U.S. Labor Markets

LAURA DRESSER

Any urban labor market is a complex and dynamic system. We summarize and describe them with careful attention to the actions and choices of individuals inside these markets—workers, students, employers, recruiters, and teachers. But the outcomes of any labor market are not simply the result of the individual and firm maximization that drives the unfettered forces of supply and demand. While our focus is often on individual outcomes generated by the "invisible hand," the context and rules of that labor market are established through the more visible but often overlooked hand of policy. Our public regulatory and legislative approaches to labor standards, worker safety laws, collective bargaining rights, employment discrimination, and civil rights all establish the rules and boundaries of the labor market. These are the most obvious and direct policies that shape our labor markets. But beyond these, broad policies on immigration, incarceration, and social welfare benefits directly shape supply in the labor market as well. Further, and less evident, are all the ways that our public framework has avoided or neglected specific issues or simply run behind, unable to catch up with new issues in the very structure, definition, and distribution of work. This chapter focuses on the context that surrounds, supports, and impedes individual and firm action in the labor market. I explore the historical development of the policy framework that defines, constrains, and in every way shapes our work in this nation. I also review the current Fight for $15 campaign and its limitations, and I close with a discussion of how new labor market policies can improve opportunity and equity for workers in the United States.

THE U.S. LABOR MARKET

The U.S. post–WWII economic order established a series of premises that shape expectations to this day. The era generated broadly shared prosperity—as the economy grew overall, so did the earnings and living standards of the broad population. Economic growth was an engine of progress in standards of living and workers' pay. Growth was so aligned with compensation and living standards that one could reliably check gross domestic product (GDP) to summarize the progress not only of productivity but also of what was going into workers' wallets.

Figure 1 shows that this relationship fell apart in the 1970s. In that decade, wages and productivity decoupled, defying expectations about the payoff to growth and shattering the expectations of the inevitable economic advance of each generation of Americans. Since the 1970s, productivity has continued to grow, but total compensation is nearly stagnant. The contrast with the preceding period is stark. From 1948 until the late 1970s, growth was tied to the middle. Since then, the economy has grown, but with very little impact on compensation.

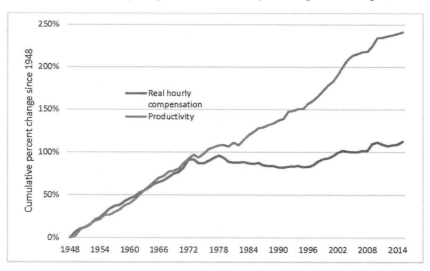

Figure 1. Cumulative Change in Total Economy Productivity and Real Hourly Compensation of Production or Nonsupervisory Workers, 1948–2015
Note: Data are for compensation of productivity of nonsupervisory workers in the private sector and net productivity of the total economy. "Net productivity" is the growth of output of goods and services less depreciation per hour worked.
Source: EPI analysis of unpublished Total Economy Productivity data from Bureau of Labor Statistics Labor Productivity and Costs program; wage data from Bureau of Labor Statistics Current Employment Statistics and Bureau of Economic Analysis National Income and Product Accounts.

As a result, economic growth has become, as one economist puts it, "a spectator sport." Despite productivity advances and increasing education of the workforce over the last quarter of a century, median wages have stagnated or have only slightly increased for some workers, and have even fallen for some groups. Families have responded by increasing their commitment to the paid labor market, with women more and more frequently working full-time in order to keep the family income up. For this last generation, women's work has provided the increase in income that economic growth no longer provides. Looking forward, that strategy is nearly exhausted (as are the parents in many of the families that have pursued it).

Some have called this decoupling the Great Divergence. It is worth noting that this picture implies growing inequality, another of the key trends generated in the labor market. Why? If the total value of goods and services in the economy has grown, and the average wage of workers is not on the rise, then rewards are getting delivered, but not through paychecks. And those rewards are going increasingly to the wealthiest in the nation.

Explaining and understanding the great divergence and the stagnation of wages has been a central project of economists for decades. It is clear that inequality is on the rise within and across most groups, that those with greater education have faired better, and that inequality is on the rise across the globe in developed economies from the United States and beyond. But the United States stands out for both the rate of increase and for the level—we lead in inequality in developed nations. Two trends most commonly named for contributing to growing inequality include rapidly changing technology and increasing globalization. These are forces that reach equally across the globe. So these drivers of inequality are shared. They can explain some of the increase in inequality in the United States.

But the growth in inequality is more rapid in the United States than elsewhere, and this extra inequality cannot be blamed on globalization or technology. Our excess inequality owes to the nation's unique institutional arrangements in labor markets. Specifically, many of the institutions that supported workers in the United States and that continue to support workers in other developed nations are in decline here. We do not have an institutional infrastructure that helps secure more broadly shared prosperity. The U.S. approach to labor markets is remarkably laissez faire, the structures that represent workers are singularly weak, and the dependence of workers on the outcomes that the labor market produces is more direct. In each of these ways, the U.S. approach to labor markets appears to be exacerbating trends toward inequality, rather than working to rein them in.

The context surrounding, constraining, reshaping, and redirecting forces of supply and demand in the United States are unique. Three seem especially important to identify. First, quality of life for workers in the United States is more directly tied to jobs than in other developed nations, where social insurance—notably health care but also paid parental leave and vacation—is guaranteed by the state. In the United States, these benefits are part of the job package, and they are worth more for workers who earn more, and nonexistent for workers at the other extreme of the labor market. So U.S. employees are, in this way, more reliant on their jobs (especially if the job offers decent health insurance), and those with better jobs tend to have better benefits. Second, the U.S. labor market is more laissez faire in the relative freedom of employers to hire and fire workers and to reshape their work. Workers are hired and fired "at will," hours of work are not guaranteed, and pay levels are entirely at the employer's discretion. While civil-rights laws create protected classes of workers who cannot be fired for reasons of, say, race or gender, these laws do not reframe the fundamental right of employers to at-will employment. And finally, and perhaps most important, the U.S. labor market is unique in having a relatively weak role for unions from the firm to the societal level. Union contracts now cover just 7.4 percent of private-sector jobs (down from 16 percent in the 1980s). Public-sector unionization rates are much higher—39 percent coverage in 2015—but its political vulnerability is evident, for example, in recent legislation in Wisconsin that makes public-sector unionization there harder as well.[1]

The policy environment around the U.S. labor market stands out among developed nations. Social insurance and job protections are weaker, and institutions representing workers interests are substantially weaker. The United States lags in these ways, and these deficits go part way to explaining why this country also stands out for the growth in inequality.

Figure 2 shows unionization and inequality in the United States over time. It is evident here that the period of increasing union density corresponded with declines in inequality. But as unions have declined, the share of income that goes to the top 10 percent has grown. This serves as a reminder of the many ways that unions can work in an economy. First, and most obvious, unions matter narrowly to the workers who are members. By negotiating wages and working conditions, union members consistently make more than nonunion workers in the economy. But as union density grows in specific sectors, the benefits to union membership begin to spill over to nonunion workers in the sector, as well. For example, compared to housekeepers in cities with few unionized hotels, hotel housekeepers in cities with high hotel union density have higher wages *regardless* of whether they clean a union property or not.[2] Density here raises the wages of all workers in the sector. And finally, unions also often pursue and support economic policies for shared prosperity. So as unions decline, their capacity to improve workers' wages, to raise floors in specific sectors, and to improve the policy environment declines as well. The decline of unions feeds the forces of inequality just as the rise of unions helps build systems that secure shared prosperity.

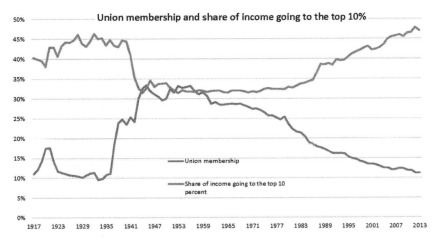

Figure 2. Union Membership and Share of Income Going to the Top 10 Percent
Source: Will Kimball and Lawrence Mishell, "Unions' Decline and the Rise of the Top 10 Percent's Share of Income," Economic Snapshot, Economic Policy Institute, February 3, 2015, accessed April 25, 2017, www.epi.org/publication/unions-decline-and-the-rise-of -the-top-10-percents-share-of-income/.

THE RISE AND FALL OF WORK REGULATION

It is worth digging into the question of how labor market regulation has evolved in the United States over the last century. Employer strategies are always emerging in response to competitive pressures and technology but also in response to the regulatory environment. Employers in turn reshape the competitive and policy terrain. With my coauthors in the introductory chapter to *The Gloves-Off Economy: Workplace Standards at the Bottom of America's Labor Market*, I trace the arc of regulation of the labor market, especially as it relates to the bottom of that labor market. (This section draws heavily on that chapter.) We argue that there are at least four ways employer norms and standards have been undermined in recent decades. First, business has become less inclined toward self-regulation. Second, government regulation of business has increasingly gone unenforced. Third, the decline in unions has limited civil-society regulation of business. And finally, the government has reduced the social-safety net and adopted policies that expand the group of vulnerable workers. In contrast to a period of rising regulation of work, recent years have moved toward deregulation. But to see the decline in regulation, it is critical first to understand the policy framework established up to the mid-1970s.[3]

RISING WORK REGULATION, 1890–1975

The regulation of employment in the United States actually emerged from businesses themselves. Growing companies began standardizing hiring and supervision, rather than leaving them to the whims of individual managers. The combination of large companies, the importance of firm-specific knowledge, and personnel management oriented toward adding value rather than cutting costs led to widespread development of internal labor markets featuring long-term employment, upward mobility, and company-run training. This business strategy was responding not only to internal priorities but also to labor unrest and union pressure from the outside.

At the same time, government regulation of employment began to develop alongside business self-regulation. Political leaders were spurred to action by the muckraking journalists and crusading advocates of the Progressive Era. States led in the innovation, instituting workers' compensation, regulating child labor, and passing safety and women's minimum-wage legislation. In the 1930s, states developed the first unemployment insurance programs.

In the crucible of the Great Depression, the federal government finally stepped forward to establish a concerted system of employer regulation via the New Deal legislation of the 1930s. The cornerstone of this system was the 1938 Fair Labor Standards Act (FLSA), which set the floor for wages and overtime. Initially, the FLSA excluded some groups of workers, but it was expanded from the 1940s through the 1980s to include most workers except for employees of state and local government, small-farm workers, and some domestic and home-care workers. The 1935 National Labor Relations Act (NLRA) provided private-sector workers with the right to organize around working conditions, to bargain collectively, and to strike.

Later, Title 7 of the 1964 Civil Rights Act prohibited discrimination by covered employers (still with a small number of exclusions, such as the federal government itself) on the basis of race, color, religion, sex, or national origin. Legislative and judicial extensions of the act banned sexual harassment and discrimination on the basis of pregnancy, age, or disability.

Finally, the regulation of health and safety on the job was established by the 1970 Occupational Safety and Health Act, which is enforced by the Occupational Safety and Health Administration (OSHA). In step with heightened government regulation of the terms and conditions of employment, civil society expanded its regulatory role as well. Labor unions took the lead.

The critical turning point for the country's labor movement came with the organizing drives of the Congress of Industrial Organizations (CIO)—and of the American Federation of Labor (AFL) from which it had emerged—in the 1930s and 1940s. In 1935, when the NLRA was passed, the AFL (prior to the CIO's departure) claimed 2.5 million members. By 1945, the AFL and CIO combined claimed 14.8 million workers, over one-third of the nonagricultural workforce.

A less widely recognized element of civil-society regulation of the workplace was launched in 1974 with the federal government's creation of the Legal Services Corporation (LSC). LSC disburses federal funds to independent local groups of public interest attorneys, with a mission to "promote equal access to justice and to provide high-quality civil legal assistance to low-income Americans."[4] While local legal-services agencies address a wide range of issues, their portfolio typically includes labor, both through individual lawsuits and through litigation directed more broadly at the implementation of "the unemployment system, wage and hour laws, low wage worker protections, and training for disadvantaged families," as one such organization describes its reach.[5]

In addition to direct regulation of employment, government took on a stronger role in regulating labor supply from about 1930. From the 1930s to the 1970s, regulating labor supply chiefly meant limiting the extent to which economically vulnerable workers were forced into taking any job, regardless of the pay, working conditions, or family needs. The 1935 Social Security Act was the key law in this regard, creating income streams for several distinct groups—widows and single mothers, the elderly, the disabled, and those unemployed through no fault of their own—to protect them from destitution when they could not work. The net effect of the act was to provide income to vulnerable groups in the workforce, making them less desperate for work.

Immigration policy can also directly expand or contract the number of vulnerable workers in an economy. For example, during a critical two decades, 1942 to 1964, the U.S. Bracero Program managed a large flow of legal, regulated immigrants from Mexico. The program, aimed at limiting illegal immigration and meeting the labor needs of agribusiness (which faced labor shortages during World War II), offered 4.5 million work contracts to Mexicans over its lifetime, about two hundred thousand each year. Braceros had far from full rights as workers: they were temporary and tied to an individual employer, and they often suffered abuse at the hands of farm owners and the U.S. and Mexican governments.

Thus, regulation of the U.S. workplace followed an upward arc for the first three-quarters of the twentieth century. Businesses built rules and bureaucracies that reshaped jobs, and an important subset of companies achieved market dominance and shared some of the resulting "rents" with their workforce. Government took an increasingly active role in mandating and enforcing employment rights and standards; civil society, especially in the form of unions, did the same.

To be sure, much of the federal policy framework was exclusionary and narrow, and, frankly, racist at its roots. The exclusions from protection of specific occupations—for example, domestic workers and farmworkers—were often concessions to the southern white political leaders who sought to lock black workers out of social protections.

Even so, government policies also provided supports and opportunities that moderated the whip of desperation for particular groups of potential workers. American workplaces in the early 1970s were no workers' paradise, but many were sheltered by a set of norms and regulations that, from today's vantage point, look quite impressive.

DECLINING WORK REGULATION AFTER 1975

Starting in the mid-1970s, business self-organization moved in new directions and the policy infrastructure began to unravel. Whereas vertical integration characterized most of the twentieth century, disintegration has been a business watchword since the 1980s. Corporations are increasingly subcontracting and outsourcing work, creating extended supply chains, and concentrating on their core competencies.[6]

The public sector as well has turned to subcontracting, in the privatization trend that swept governments from federal to local in recent decades. Globalization and rapid technological change have rendered market dominance more transitory. Capital has become more mobile, undermining job stability and workers' bargaining power.

Businesses draw increasingly on nonstandard forms of work, often mediated by a third party: even the largest corporations have distanced themselves from lifetime employment.[7] As AT&T geared up to lay off an estimated forty thousand workers in early 1996, Vice President for Human Resources James Meadows told the New York Times that "people need to look at themselves as self-employed, as vendors who come to this company to sell their skills." Instead of "jobs," people increasingly have "projects" or "fields of work," he remarked, leading to a society that is increasingly "jobless but not workless."[8] This remark, surprising in the 1990s, is a common perception regarding work in the twenty-first century.

How did the policy environment change? Part of the shift arose from policy makers hostile to the idea of regulations. Beginning with President Reagan in 1981, Republican presidents began salting the National Labor Relations Board with people opposed to unions. At the same time, industries such as restaurants and retail, which employ the bulk of low-wage workers, led the drive to reduce the real value of the minimum wage.

Another factor is the spread of new forms of business organization, such as subcontracting. While construction and apparel industries have used subcontractors for decades, the practice has now become so broadly prevalent that entire new industries have arisen—from security services to food preparation, janitorial services to call centers. Radio ads often air offering accountants and other office "temps"—one ad even playing on the fears of full-time employees being replaced by the more efficient temporary worker.

Elsewhere, strong-arm approaches by employers to fight off union drives took a toll. For example, employers threaten to close all or part of their business in more than half of all union organizing campaigns. Unions win only 38 percent of representation elections when such threats are made, compared to 51 percent when there are no such threats. Deunionization in the construction, trucking, and garment industries has led to greater fracturing of work and degradation of job quality for workers in those industries.

With unions on the defensive and reduced to a shrinking corner of the private sector, employers have had a relatively free hand. The gap between union and nonunion compensation yawns wide. Full-time workers who are union members earn 30 percent more per week than their nonunion counterparts. While 70 percent of union workers have defined-benefit pension plans; only 15 percent of nonunion workers do. Perhaps most important, the decline in union strength has meant more relaxed observance of labor and safety codes, fueling downward spirals in wage standards and working conditions that ultimately make life harder—and more dangerous—for workers.

Federal enforcement of labor standards and occupational safety is also falling behind new organization and the ever expanding U.S. labor market. The Brennan Center for Justice reports that between 1975 and 2004, the number of federal workplace investigators declined by 14 percent and compliance-actions completed dropped by 36 percent. At the same time, the number of workers covered by federal workplace protections increased 55 percent and the number of covered workplaces grew by 112 percent. The OSHA budget has been cut by $14.5 million since 2001, and the department's focus under the Bush administration shifted from enforcement and deterrence to "compliance assistance." At 2004 staffing and inspection levels, it would take OSHA 133 years to visit each workplace under its jurisdiction just once.

GROWTH IN VULNERABLE WORKER POPULATIONS

Intentionally or not, federal and state policy makers exacerbated these trends in enforcement by adopting policies that left a growing number of workers vulnerable in our labor market. The dimensions of this include immigration policy, safety-net and welfare policy, and criminal-justice and incarceration policy.

Widely regarded as dysfunctional on a host of dimensions, U.S. immigration policy has effectively increased the number of workers vulnerable to gloves-off strategies, because undocumented workers are largely unable to access core rights in the workplace. Sometimes these workers do not know of the basic protections that the U.S. labor market extends to all workers. Sometimes the threat of deportation is all it takes to keep them from demanding the rights they know they have. In either case, their status undermines their bargaining position in the labor market. In particular, the 1986 Immigration Reform and Control Act legalized nearly 3 million immigrants but simultaneously criminalized the knowing employment of undocumented immigrants. This criminalization, coupled with escalating enforcement of employer sanctions consigns some 11 million undocumented workers to a shadowy existence without status and vulnerable to workplaces abuses. The 2002 U.S. Supreme Court Hoffman Plastic Compounds decision made things worse, as the first recent decision to chip away undocumented immigrants' recourse to formal protection under law.[9]

In addition, paralysis in immigration policy, federal welfare reform and mass incarceration have also added to the pool of vulnerable workers. Welfare reform of 1996 practically eliminated financial support for nonworking single mothers pushing millions into the labor pool, often trapping them in low-wage jobs and leaving them vulnerable to abuse.[10] Beyond those women are other low-wage workers who may have stood up for their own rights or bargained for decent treatment if they knew they could count on some public support if they lost their job. The loss of the fallback option reduces security for those workers too. Other social programs were hard hit by the shift toward reducing the social wage. Unemployment insurance today reaches a smaller proportion of the unemployed than it did thirty or forty years ago: whereas in 1970, 44 percent of the unemployed received unemployment insurance, in 2006 that percentage had fallen to 35 percent.[11]

And finally, surging incarceration rates have created a mushrooming ex-offender population that faces significant formal and informal bars to employment. As of 2008, 2.2 million persons, disproportionately black and Latino, were behind bars, a 500 percent increase over the previous thirty years.[12] The United States has the highest incarceration rate of any nation in the Organization for Economic Co-operation and Development, much of which stems from the high rates of incarceration for drug offenses. As they are released from prison, ex-offenders face significant challenges integrating into stable employment, especially since many more sectors of the labor market now use background checks and limit employment for felons, pushing yet another population to the margins of the world of work. The evidence of discrimination against workers with criminal records, especially black formerly incarcerated men, is powerful.[13]

From immigrants with too few documents to community residents returning from prisons with too long a record, public policy is contributing to vulnerability in labor markets.

RECENT PROGRESS IN RAISING STANDARDS

The trajectory of labor standards is not a simple downward spiral of declining regulation, however. Advocates, organizers, policy makers, and even some employers are developing new strategies around job quality. Inequality is in the news, and the struggles of the U.S. middle class is at the center of political debates. The Fight for $15 has brought the minimum wage back to the political forefront with substantial wage increases in store for some 17 million workers. Comprehensive immigration reform remains a priority of business groups and some political leaders. The Obama administration deployed executive orders to extend opportunity or strengthen coverage of labor law. By late 2016 the minimum wage for federal workers was up, home health workers previously exempted from labor standards were now included, and the nation's overtime rules had been updated to cover more workers. After distressing General Accounting Office audits from the early 2000s showed that the Department of Labor rarely enforced labor law, under the Obama administration enforcement was reactivated, extended, and focused.

FIGHT FOR $15

Born of New York City fast-food strikes in late 2012, the Fight for $15 has become a powerful force for labor standards and minimum-wage increases. Fast food workers in cities across the nation walked off their jobs to draw attention to the fact that they simply could not survive at the minimum wage. The movement gained momentum as other workers began to rally to the call for $15 per hour and a union. Retail and other food service workers, child care workers and home health aides, and adjunct faculty all joined the fight.

While the original slogan of campaigns "$15 and a union" implied a focus on bargaining wage increases, over time the most active and effective front in the fight has been the minimum wage. Early on, the level was perceived by many (even some on the left) to be impossibly aggressive and perhaps even economically destructive. Skeptics noted that $15 per hour wasn't so very far from the median wage nationally (42 percent of workers earn $15 or less), and $15 exceeds the median in many rural labor markets. In some states, the minimum wages was moving to around $10 per hour, and few negative effects were being documented (indeed, the states with higher minimum wages have posted faster job growth in recent years). But $15 was unchartered territory, and analysts and political leaders were wary.

But despite the skepticism, the movement caught fire. Substantial wage increases were passed by cities all across the nation. Seattle, San Francisco, and Los Angeles and dozens of other cities all embraced $15. In 2016, two of the nation's largest states, New York and California, followed suit. To be sure, these wages are not moving overnight. Most laws have schedules, with the final steps still a few years in the future. But what once seemed impossible has become a political reality. Some 17 million workers will eventually benefit from minimum-wage increases that have been spurred on by the Fight for $15. Of those, 10 million are already on their way to $15.[14]

This success is changing the wages of workers across the country. It has also transformed the national conversation on minimum wages. The federal minimum wage, stuck at $7.25 per hour and less than half the $15 that is spreading, now seems even more absurdly low. The Democratic platform in 2016 embraced $15 per hour. Simultaneously, in recent years, many employers, major retailers Walmart and Target among them, announced wage increases that move their entry-level workers well above the minimum wage. Polling and referenda demonstrate enormous support across the political spectrum for substantial increases.

In 2012, when the first fry cooks and cashiers walked off their jobs, none of this progress seemed plausible. The audacious demand for a significant raise, growing concern about inequality and opportunity in the nation, the clear inability to make ends meet on such low wages, and worker leadership and smart organizing strategies all came together and changed what was possible.

The Fight for $15 is the most exciting and effective movement around labor standards in the nation today. Even so, the limitations of the fight indicate two serious problems that will riddle any strategy to improve labor standards through policy.

STANDARDS IN A TIME OF POLITICAL POLARIZATION

In the face of ongoing failure of the federal government to raise the minimum wage, the fight moved to the states and cities. As the movement caught hold, cities especially proved fertile ground. Given the high cost of living, observable wealth inequities, and progressive coalitions in cities, the argument for increases and the political muscle to secure them were more readily available there. Once cities began to pass ordinances, others followed suit and something of a public-policy race to the top was started. In fact, the two states mentioned earlier, New York and California, passed $15 at a state level on the same day.

But this works, of course, in liberal enclaves—urban America is certainly more liberal, but not every city is pursuing wage increases. Only two states have stepped up to $15, and other states may follow suit. But it is relatively easy to anticipate where steps forward will be made and where the federal minimum will hold sway. In the Northeast and West Coast, minimum wages are systematically above the federal level already. In some states, those wages will grow more rapidly. But in the South and the Great Plains, the Fight for $15 will not have as much traction and support. Some cities attempting to raise wages will find their authority taken away by conservative state legislatures, as happened when the state of Alabama passed legislation to preempt Montgomery from raising wages.

The result of this dynamic will almost certainly be a growing gap in the regulatory infrastructure and labor market standards of liberal states compared to conservative states. This is not a reason to resist the change, but a caution about its limits. And the diversity of approaches will build evidence and evaluative insights on the economic impact of these strategies, and that evidence may help leverage change in other states. But it is worth remembering that this strategy has substantially less promise for workers in conservative states. Like their counterparts across the nation, fast-food workers across Wisconsin have gone on strike. The movement for them has been instructive and the success elsewhere has been inspiring, but the inability to see any possible change in the state takes its toll.

Conservatives' strong and consistent focus on undermining labor standards and union rights is the flip side of the success of the Fight for $15: right to work, the weakening of public-sector unions, state preemption of minimum wage or paid sick leave legislation at the local level, reductions in unemployment insurance. The playbook in red states tends to move those states down in labor standards even as the Fight for $15 is raising the floor in more liberal states. At the state level, labor market regimes are diverging and the gap between states is growing. This divergence will leave some workers behind and make federal policy ever harder to calibrate.

WAGE STANDARDS AND THE FUTURE OF WORK

When the job is clear and the employer well defined, raising the minimum wage is the most direct policy approach to raising labor standards. For the vast majority of U.S. workers, the job and the employer are clear and definable, so raising the minimum wage is direct and effective.

But workers can be left out of wage increases and many have been. Most obvious here is the long-standing differential treatment of tipped workers. The federal minimum wage for tipped workers is just $2.13 per hour. Tipped workers clear the minimum through their tips, at least in theory. But wage increases that do not attend to this vast exclusion or raise wages for tipped workers are leaving many behind. States are increasingly taking this issue on. In eight states, the state's minimum wage applies to tipped workers.

Beyond this sort of policy exclusion, the minimum wage simply does not apply to the "self-employed" and "independent contractors." For example, care work, both in home health care and family-provided child care, is often structured in ways that put hundreds of thousands of low-wage workers outside the influence of minimum-wage increases. Especially in home health, these jobs are growing rapidly because of aging populations and health care system restructuring. States arrange this work in different ways, but in many states, these home health workers are treated as independent contractors. For independent contractors and the self-employed, the minimum wage simply does not pertain.

Further, it is clear that workers have seen a shift to "independent contractor" in a number of other industries. Trucking has been transformed to an industry dominated by "independent contractors." That many truckers work for only one company and that companies determine the conditions of the work is strong evidence that this work is not truly "independent." In construction the practice of misclassification of workers is pervasive, as well. It is very hard to get numbers on this, but the data available suggest that this is on the rise. In Massachusetts, the misclassification of workers as independent contractors climbed from 8 percent in 1995 to 19 percent in 2003.[15]

This is of increasing relevance looking forward, as well. The "future of work" is often imagined as a "gig" economy, where workers are managing their employment with multiple employers, mediated through technology. Uber is the obvious example here. And the actual employment status of Uber drivers (independent contractors vs. Uber employees) remains an open and contentious legal question. To the extent that such drivers and similar workers are defined as "independent contractors," the strategy of improving the labor market by raising the minimum wage misses the mark.

Remember that in the United States social provision is much more tied to work. This is true in health insurance, obviously, but also in the provision of everything from sick leave to retirement. While other developed economies often have more social approaches to these standards, in the United States, all of this is delivered through "jobs." To the extent that the future of work will generate people doing work, but not doing that work in "jobs," the U.S. economy will leave those workers with little access to basic social provision. Developed nations that deliver social provisions of health and retirement outside of the context of the "job" will be better positioned for this evolution.

The idea of a basic income—provision of basic income regardless of work—is an emerging answer to the concern about the future of work. While the conversation remains largely theoretical and politically remote in the United States, there is more active consideration in Europe. Indeed, Swiss voters rejected a basic income plan in the summer of 2016. But the conversation continues to simmer. And in Finland and the Netherlands, experiments in basic income are underway.

TOWARD A PUBLIC LABOR STANDARDS POLICY

Public policies, those relating directly to labor market regulation and those relating directly to workers' vulnerability in labor markets, are the foundational structure for how firms and workers interact. Since the 1980s, that balance has tipped more strongly in favor or employers, perhaps especially at the bottom of the labor market.

The recovery from the Great Recession, the Fight for $15, and the Obama administration strengthening of labor markets through administrative rules are all steps toward restoring a more equitable balance in labor markets. These steps, and further steps, will necessarily reactivate or extend government regulation while building civic- or work-based infrastructure, like unions, that can uphold and pursue worker interests at the shop floor and in the broader political context. This may not always look like traditional unions. For example, immigrant worker centers are giving low-wage workers a means to organize outside of the traditional union framework.

The priority in this endeavor will be to help fix an economic system that rewards employers who break the law and punishes those who try to play by the rules. This is a moment for potentially great change in the way our society operates. Workers, government, unions, and responsible employers all have a stake in finding ways to strengthen the policy framework around the U.S. labor market.

A few principles may help frame this project:

- A strong and well-enforced labor market floor is good for the economy
- Organized workers can be a force for production and productivity
- Employer and public supports need to be mutually reinforcing
- A stronger labor market infrastructure requires public investment and public policy

I take each of these in turn.

A strong and well-enforced labor market floor is good for the economy. The institutions that support a strong labor market—unions, minimum wage laws, basic labor standards, and public enforcement infrastructure to aggressively enforce them—are often criticized as impediments to competition. From this viewpoint, strengthening labor standards is simply inefficient, generating costs on firms, limiting employment opportunity for disadvantaged workers, and choking economic growth. Business associations, some economists, and conservative political leaders all rely on these sorts of arguments when resisting minimum-wage raises or increases in other labor standards.

The research on the economic impact of minimum-wage increases, however, does not confirm these dire predictions. Since the mid-1990s, when economists studying a minimum-wage increase found no negative employment impact in fast-food employment, an increasing body of research supports the idea that stronger labor standards do not undermine low-wage labor markets.

Beyond the narrower question of employment impact, there are important dynamics in labor markets that higher standards may actually support.

First, note that higher minimum-wage and benefits standards, and stronger enforcement of those standards, do not impact all businesses equally. The employers at or beneath the floor have the most to lose when standards go up. Raising the floor and enforcing it levels the playing field for higher-wage firms. For example, in construction when some contractors begin to misclassify their workers as independent contactors (and thereby lower their wage bill by avoiding workers' compensation and unemployment insurance that are the due of workers), those contractors undermine the ability of other contractors to win bids. They create a downward pressure on all employers in the sector by avoiding or evading labor law and standards. Strong, well-enforced labor standards can help firms compete on more fair footing.

Organized workers can be a force for production and productivity. One reason that stronger labor standards can be good for the economy is that moving wages to a more livable level can help stabilize the workforce, increase productivity, and decrease the high costs of employee turnover. This is a first instance of this principle that organized and rewarded workers can become a force for production.

In any sector, there is more than one way to organize work. Some firms may take a low-wage, high-turnover approach, while others may pursue a higher-wage approach. The higher-wage firm pays more for labor and is rewarded with loyalty, reduced turnover costs, and higher-quality production. In most sectors, there is no single production system or way of organizing work—instead, there are multiple competitive approaches. While more than one approach may be competitive, some approaches are unambiguously better for workers and communities. Roughly characterized as "high-road" firms, the companies that compete with a greater focus on quality and value added generally also invest in and hold onto their workers. They compete against "low-road" firms more focused on cost reduction including holding down wages. While either system is competitive, one approach is unambiguously better for workers and communities. Pursuing broadly shared prosperity requires closing off low-road choices (e.g., raising the minimum wage), making the high road more available (e.g., supporting industrial modernization), and building systems and infrastructure that help workers and firms move to the high road. To do so requires acknowledging the important contributions of workers and rewarding their work.

Employer and public supports need to be mutually reinforcing. Too often employer standards and public supports are thought of as alternative approaches to solving labor market problems. This happens when pundits present the Earned Income Tax Credit as a more efficient alternative to the minimum wage. In fact, however, these are not policy alternatives, but mutually reinforcing structures. Without strong private labor standards, the public can get stuck with an increasingly costly redistribution for workers paid too little to actually make ends meet. Key employers and sectors are called out in reports that calculate the high public costs of low-wage jobs. A destructive example of this is when a new firm enters an industry and decides to stop offering health insurance (or offer a very weak or expensive policy only). Other firms in the sector want to remain price competitive; they find they must reduce the quality of their health insurance package to keep up. Competitive pressure can thereby undermine labor standards. But in the worst case, not only do labor standards fall, but workers increasingly seek public health insurance (through state programs funded by Medicaid) to make up for the losses in employer-based health insurance. And in this way, the sector is undermined and public costs grow.

Public supports for the working poor, like Medicaid and FoodShare, need to be understood to be a compliment to higher labor standards. Stronger standards help keep the pubic cost of those programs down. Stronger enforcement of standards helps reward the many employers who have been doing the right thing, rather than subsidizing the very employers that are undermining standards in the first place.

Stronger labor market infrastructure requires public investment and public policy. Stronger labor market infrastructure will require real public investment and consistent attention to the intended and indirect labor market consequences of policy. This is perhaps obvious, but is worth stating in this current political moment with its attendant focus of austerity in budgets and curtailment of government services. Though we often seem trapped in a debate that scapegoats immigrants and rejects refugees, we need to develop and support a national political conversation on upholding labor standards for all workers. Rather than trying to eliminate workers' access to unemployment insurance, we need to build a more robust system of support for workers and communities devastated by economic restructuring. To build a stronger labor market infrastructure of supports for workers and to enforce a stronger set of standards for employers will require substantial public investment as well as a shift in political winds toward a greater appreciation for that investment.

CONCLUSION

Essentially, I argue that stronger labor standards could actually be good for the economy. Not just for the workers who earn higher wages, but for the entire labor market, firms and workers alike. The authors of *How Big Should Our Government Be?* make the argument even more broadly: "more government can lead to greater security, enhanced opportunity and a fairer sharing of national wealth."[16] They argue that the government should be investing in infrastructure and expanding social insurance. To do so requires it to be larger than it is, but to do so also embraces growth and security and more broadly shared prosperity. This is an essentially optimistic point. The United States could restore broadly shared prosperity, but it will require government infrastructure to do so.

Some of the work to improve the labor market is already underway. At the forefront is the movement to raise the minimum wage. But activists and policy leaders are pursuing other policy fronts: mandatory sick leave, paid family leave insurance, and the regulation of work time to make hours of low-wage workers more predictable. Like the minimum wage, these changes in labor standards will emerge in cities and states first, bubbling up to the national discussion. Activists and leaders are also increasingly seeking ways to secure rights and opportunity for all—regardless of immigration status or incarceration history—at the state and local level. As these innovations are documented and evaluated, the concrete case for expanding labor standards and strengthening workers rights will be developed at the local level and inform innovation across the nation.

Notes

1. Barry T. Hirsch and David A. Macpherson, *Union Membership and Earnings Data Book: Compilations from the Current Population Survey*, 2016 ed. (N.p.: Bloomberg and Bureau of National Affairs, 2016).

2. Annette Bernhardt, Laura Dresser, and Erin Hatton, "The Coffee Pot Wars: Unions and Firm Restructuring in the Hotel Industry," in *Low-Wage America: How Employers are Reshaping Opportunity in the Workplace*, ed. Eileen Appelbaum, Annette Bernhardt, and Richard J. Murnane (New York: Russel Sage Foundation, 2003), 33–76.

3. Annette D. Bernhardt, Heather Boushey, Laura Dresser, and Chris Tilly, introduction to *The Gloves-Off Economy: Workplace Standards at the Bottom of America's Labor Market* (Berkeley: Institute for Research on Labor and Employment, 2008).

4. "Who We Are," Legal Services Corporation, 2008, accessed October 19, 2016, www.lsc.gov/about-lsc/who-we-are.

5. "Legal Issues," Greater Boston Legal Services, accessed October 19, 2016, www.gbls.org/get-legal-help/legal-issues.

6. Gary Gereffi, "The Global Economy: Organization, Governance, and Development," in *Handbook of Economic Sociology*, ed. Neil Smelser and Richard Swedberg

(Princeton, NJ: Princeton University Press, 2003), 160–82. Bennett Harrison, *Lean and Mean: The Changing Landscape of Corporate Power in the Age of Flexibility* (New York: Basic Books, 1994). Philip Moss, Harold Salzman, and Chris Tilly, "Limits to Market-Mediated Employment: From Deconstruction to Reconstruction of Internal Labor Markets" in *Non-Traditional Work Arrangements and the Changing Labor Market: Dimensions, Causes, and Institutional Responses,* ed. Francoise Carré, Marianne Ferber, Lonnie Golden, and Steve Herzenberg (Madison, WI: Industrial Relations Research Association, 2000), 95–121.

7. William Baumol, Alan S. Blinder, and Edward N. Wolff, *Downsizing in America: Reality, Causes, and Consequences* (New York: Russell Sage Foundation, 2003).

8. Edmund L. Andrews, "Don't Go Away Mad, Just Go Away: Can AT&T Be the Nice Guy as It Cuts 40,000 Jobs?," *New York Times*, February 13, 1996, D10.

9. Sarah Gammage, "Working on the Margins: Migration and Employment in the United States," in Bernhardt et al., *Gloves-Off Economy*, 137–61; Amy Sugimori, "State and Local Policy Models Promoting Immigrant Worker Justice," in ibid., 217–42.

10. Elizabeth Lower-Basch and Mark H. Greenberg, "Single Mothers in the Era of Welfare Reform," in Bernhardt et al., *Gloves-Off Economy*, 163–89.

11. Department of Labor, Employment Standards Administration, Wage and Hour Division, "History of Changes to the Minimum Wage Law," accessed October 19, 2016, www.dol.gov/whd/minwage/coverage.htm; Executive Office of the President and Council of Economic Advisors, "Economic Report of the President," Washington: United States Government Printing Office, 2007, www.gpo.gov.

12. "Criminal Justice Facts," Sentencing Project, 2008, accessed April 25, 2017, www.sentencingproject.org/criminal-justice-facts/.

13. Devah Pager, "The Mark of a Criminal Record," *American Journal of Sociology* 108, no. 5 (2003), 937–75.

14. "Fight for $15 Impact Report Fact Sheet," National Employment Law Project, April 12, 2016, accessed April 25, 2017, www.nelp.org/publication/fight-for-15-impact-report-raises-for-17-million-workers-10-million-going-to-15/.

15. Francoise Carré and Randall Wilson, "The Social and Economic Costs of Employee Misclassification in Construction," Construction Policy Research Center, Harvard Law School Labor and Worklife Program and Harvard School of Public Health (Cambridge: MA, 2004), accessed April 25, 2017, www.law.harvard.edu/programs/lwp/Misclassification%20Report%20Mass.pdf.

16. Jon Bakija, Lane Kenworthy, Peter Lindert, and Jeff Madrick, *How Big Should Our Government Be?* (Oakland: University of California Press, 2016), x.

Immigration to the United States in the Post–Civil Rights Years

XÓCHITL BADA

The United States has seen two massive waves of immigration since the late nineteenth century: 27.6 million immigrants arrived between 1881 and 1930, and then, after a slowdown of immigrant flows of more than three decades due to restrictive immigration policies of the 1920s, the Depression era, and World War II, a modern immigration wave doubled the immigrant population compared to that of the early twentieth century. By 2015, fifty years after the passage of the immigration law that reconfigured U.S. immigration policy, nearly 59 million immigrants have arrived, reconfiguring the social and economic landscape of urban and rural places across the United States.

In 1960, the foreign-born population represented about 1 in 20 residents, mostly from countries in Europe who had settled in the Northeast and Midwest. By 2015, the foreign-born population reached 14 percent of the total population: 45 million, the vast majority (53%) coming from Latin America, mostly from Mexico, El Salvador, Cuba, Dominican Republic, and Guatemala.[1] Among post-1965 immigrants, one-quarter came from Asia. As a consequence of new foreign-born arrivals and their U.S.-born children, the Latino share of the U.S. population rose from 4 percent in 1965 to 18 percent in 2015. Asians also saw their share rise, from less than 1 percent in 1965 to 6 percent in 2015.

The nation's Latino population, which was 35.5 million in 2000, grew 43 percent over the past decade. The Latino population accounted for most of the nation's growth—56 percent—from 2000 to 2010.[2] This population is still heavily concentrated; 76 percent live in nine states with long-standing historical communities (Arizona, California, Colorado, Florida, Illinois, New

Mexico, New Jersey, New York, and Texas), although the share living in other states is growing.[3] While for some observers population concentration may seem to facilitate the integration of Latino immigrant communities, the dramatic demographic shifts in many of these states have led to the racialization, anti-immigrant narrative, and "raid mentality" that prevailed in national political conversations during the 2016 presidential race.[4]

While the United States is facing these difficult but important conversations about immigration management and governance, it is important to remember that by 1980, eighteen of the twenty-five most populous cities in 1950 had lost residents. Of the twenty-five largest cities in 1980s, seventeen gained residents over the subsequent thirty years. Undoubtedly, the single largest factor in this population trend reversal has been a rapid increase in the population of Latinos, who have often remained tied to central cities. Of the twenty-five largest U.S. cities, twelve have populations that are more than one-quarter Hispanic, including eight over one-third and two that are majority Latino.[5]

Among conservative politicians and their audience, one of the major hurdles to achieving comprehensive immigration reform is the resistance to offer a path to legalization to those who entered the United States without authorization. For conservatives, allowing the undocumented to pay a fine and be offered an opportunity to regularize their status if they have not violated any other laws is completely unacceptable, while liberal politicians are more likely to agree that a path to legalization is a fair solution to bring millions of undocumented out of the shadows. By and large, the successful incorporation of different racial and ethnic minorities is one of the biggest challenges that the United States has faced in the last century.

THE SECOND GREAT MIGRATION

In his book *Dream Chasers*, John Tirman compares African American internal migration with Latin American migration. In fact, post-1965 immigration from Latin America bears important similarities with the Great Migration, which leads Tirman to propose it as "the Second Great Migration." Between 1915 and the 1970s, a massive similar but internal labor migration happened from the old Confederacy to the North and the West. As Isabel Wilkerson vividly reminds us, over these six decades, 6 million African American southerners left their birthplaces to spread across the country for an uncertain journey. They moved to New York, Detroit, Chicago, Los Angeles,

Philadelphia, and smaller, equally "foreign" cities for them, such as Syracuse, Oakland, Milwaukee, Newark, and Gary.[6]

Although each of those places turned into a land of new opportunities, African Americans took considerable risks as Jim Crow laws persisted well into the 1960s. They had to face perils that many blacks found intimidating, including detention. African Americans were accepted, at least conditionally, as inexpensive labor in the northern industrial cities. In the Midwest, employers brought African Americans and Mexican immigrants as strikebreakers to undermine the organizing efforts of previous waves of European immigrant workers in meatpacking, steel manufacturing, and railroad construction. Yet, the newfound job opportunities and social conditions of African Americans were better than those in the South, and within time, the power of social networks would make sure that African Americans dispersed across the United States.

The Great Migration, which was fed by the continued mistreatment of former black slaves and their children in the South, changed the racial compositions and the social and cultural dynamics of Chicago, Detroit, New York, and other northern cities. In Chicago alone, the black population increased from 44,000 at the start of this migration to over 1 million at the end of it.[7] In comparison, the Latino migration, mainly from Mexico but also from Central America, Cuba, Puerto Rico, and the Dominican Republic, has been equal or larger in scale and as significant in reshaping parts of the country demographically, as well as shaping U.S. politics and culture. Comparing the two sheds light on the cultural resistance to Latino immigration. After half a century of official desegregation policies and civil-rights laws to bring equal opportunity to all regardless of skin color, African Americans are still marginalized and discriminated against, with similar poverty and educational attainment rates as many recently arrived immigrants from Latin America. Yet, statistics show that, in the last seventy-five years, the incomes of blacks have increased substantially relative to those of whites, and that a black middle class has taken root. Compared to the Jim Crow South, the progress is slow but undeniable.

While African Americans were fleeing sharecropping traps, grinding agricultural labor, debt peonage, scarce educational opportunities, formal segregation, and the absence of government services, many Latin American immigrants were also fleeing deteriorating economic conditions, agricultural disinvestment, dictatorships, civil wars, and natural disasters, following the lure of readily available jobs in the United States. For those immigrants, the promise of a better future has also been largely fulfilled despite persistent lags. The second generation of Latino immigrants already advances beyond its parents, but it lags behind the native-born majority of the same age and occupation. This socioeconomic disadvantage creates challenges for the social mobility of entire minority immigrant groups. For example, the 35 percent poverty rate for Latino children is almost as high as it is for black children.[8] There's no question that some sectors of the second generation are experiencing social mobility and integrating in the mainstream, but much remains to be done to improve the social mobility of immigrants and their children and to avoid pushing them into a permanent underclass.[9]

In this chapter, we present a brief overview of post-1965 immigration to the United States, including the challenges and potential opportunities that immigrants offer to the revitalization of metropolitan regions in need of advancing their positions in diverse labor markets. The aging of the baby-boom population and the need to increase productivity while keeping labor costs under control will eventually lead to the reform of current federal immigration policies, which no longer reflect the economic needs of sectors such as agriculture, that are still facing shortages of low-cost, unskilled labor to maintain consumer staples like tomatoes available to the middle class at low prices.

The nation's immigrant population increased sharply from 1970 to 2000, though the rate of growth has slowed since then. Still, the United States has the world's largest immigrant population, with one in five of the world's immigrants. Between 1965 and 2015, new immigrants, their children. and their grandchildren accounted for 55 percent of U.S. population growth. They added 72 million people to the nation's population, as it grew from 193 million in 1965 to 324 million in 2015.[10]

It is important to stress that the recent profile of the immigrant population twenty-five years and older reveals new trends suggesting a higher intensity in the growth of the population of skilled immigrants. For example, between 2006 and 2012, the immigrant population twenty-five years and older without a university degree increased 15 percent, while the immigrant population with a university degree of the same age group—the so-called qualified or skilled immigrants—increased 22.4 percent.[11] New immigration trends also suggest a feminization of the qualified migrant group, as the female percentage of qualified migrants increased 27 percent. The profile of Mexican immigration to the United States is also changing. For example, a select group of wealthy Mexicans seeking to escape violence at home have attained EB-5 visas to gain entry into the United States.[12] The number of Mexicans participating in the EB-5 program, albeit still small, has increased significantly over the last several years, with Mexico ranked seventh worldwide in EB-5 visas in 2010.[13]

SOUTH–NORTH MIGRATION AND ITS CAUSES

In the last thirty years, most of the anti-immigrant narratives and legal regulations have focused on policies aimed at deporting those already here and controlling future immigration flows, while less attention is paid to the incorporation of immigrants and their children and to addressing the root causes that lead to economic migrations. The current climate of anti-immigrant sentiment among certain sectors of the U.S. population may be explained by the substantial differences in the past immigration waves with the post-1965 one mostly because both of the U.S. immigration waves in the mid-nineteenth century and early twentieth century consisted almost entirely of European immigrants.

Due to the vibrant associational culture and the assimilationist ideology of immigrant settlement houses across the United States, successive waves of late nineteenth- and early twentieth-century European immigrants had multiple opportunities for incorporation. Interestingly, the role of local governments in the immigrant integration process has been a historically important variable. For example, during the Great Depression years, the city of Chicago did not experience a coercive repatriation program because Cook County officials denied the Immigration and Naturalization Service (INS) access to the relief lists. In that period, an estimated 20 percent of relief recipients were foreign born in Cook County, and Mayor Antonín Josef Čermák, the foreign-born Bohemian American mayor, refused to cooperate with the INS to facilitate the repatriation of low-wage Chicago immigrants.[14]

While it is true that southern Europeans were not as easily incorporated as western and northern Europeans, the majority of European immigrants and their U.S.-born children eventually achieved successful incorporation. In the case of Italians, a survey of three thousand families in Chicago in 1920 by the Illinois Health Insurance Commission found that 58 percent of Italian American families sampled had some form of life insurance, and at least half of these policies were held in Italian mutual aid societies.[15] Competition, conflict, accommodation, and assimilation—the four necessary steps that sociologist Robert Park observed to mark immigrant adaptation to the new society—were eventually accomplished by European immigrants. In fact, the classical assimilation process in the United States was mostly described using examples from European migrant communities that transformed into hyphenated ethnic Americans when their emigration flows to the United States considerably decreased.

In contrast, post-1965 immigrants have had limited opportunities to pursue social incorporation due to the limited availability of necessary social services. The growing inequalities and disempowerment that have accompanied the implementation of neoliberal agendas have resulted in the disappearance of public funds to support economic integration for disadvantaged groups living in working-class neighborhoods. A severe decline of public responsibilities and the increased privatization of critical social services have slowed down the successful incorporation of post-1965 immigrants compared to previous immigrant waves. With the exception of migrant-led hometown associations, very few organizations have been able to fill the void left by Hull House and other immigrant settlement houses after some of these institutions transformed their mission and devoted their energies to addressing the needs of refugees and other economically disadvantaged populations after the decline of Western and Northern European immigration to the United States.[16]

The social distance emerging from racial, ethnic, and class distinctions between past waves of European immigrants and their descendants and the current one bring a mix of prejudices including blaming the victim attitudes, exhortations about white superiority, and the manipulation of the rules of the game for economic advantage. Latino immigrants are changing the American dream, the culture of the Protestant white Europeans who, according to their own narrative, built the nation. In this narrative, immigrants from Latin America are fundamentally at odds with supposedly quintessential American traits such as English language ability, an ethic of hard work, and patriotism.

The U.S. Immigration Act of 1965 increased the possibilities of emigration from Latin American countries to the United States due to the elimination of the blatantly discriminatory national-origins quota system, which since the 1920s had favored migration from Northern and Western Europe and excluded Asians altogether. However, the 1965 legislation also imposed a one-size-fits-all regulation, where all countries would be limited to no more than 7 percent of the total each year, thus opening the door to a large influx of migrant workers from Latin America countries, many of them without authorization.[17]

It is not a coincidence that the largest share of Latin American migrants came mostly from countries that had experienced U.S. military interventions and occupations throughout the twentieth century. In fact, the United States was more than just these migrants' destination because it also played a role in creating the conditions in some of those countries that led them to migrate. The exile produced by the Cuban Revolution, the chronic underemployment in Puerto Rico, the 1965 U.S. military intervention in the Dominican Republican, the U.S. Congress military support to the Salvadoran Army's war against the opposition groups in the 1980s, and the agricultural unemployment created by the North American Free Trade Agreement (NAFTA) in the mid-1990s are considered some of the push factors leading workers and families to migrate to the United States in the last fifty years.[18] By and large, NAFTA was the culmination of free trade among unequal commercial partners in a region where the movement of merchandise became increasingly free while the movement of people faced enormous obstacles in a region without free labor mobility. During NAFTA's aftermath period, increased wage and income inequalities among NAFTA's three partners led to immediate displacement and uprooting in Mexico as a consequence of decreasing agricultural employment opportunities in Mexico's rural countryside.[19] In the absence of compensatory funds to alleviate the pressures created by enormous development disparities in the NAFTA region, millions of Mexicans decided to cross the northern border seeking better employment opportunities.

With few exceptions, the multiple waves of post–World War II Latin American migrants came to the United States and settled in the West and the South, finding different contexts of reception when joining previously established immigrant groups. Immigrant incorporation processes of diverse groups have been largely determined by legal status, racial identification, country of origin, and varied local contexts of reception. Many Latin American immigrants, especially Mexicans and Central Americans, came with comparatively low levels of education and fulfilled the demand of jobs in manufacturing and the service sector economy.

In Latin America, the failure of the import-substitution economic model,[20] the debt crisis of the 1980s, and growing income distribution inequality sent many workers in search of better economic opportunities.[21] While economic liberalization and free trade agreements were taking shape in Latin America, the United States was experiencing a transformation of the manufacturing sector that had provided the working class with the basic means of survival at the end of World War II, thanks to a pact between the state, workers, and unions. This pact had established an increase in productivity in exchange for sharing a small fraction of the profits with workers. However, as competitive capitalism transformed to monopoly capitalism and U.S. corporations lost their competitive advantage to Germany and Japan in the early 1970s, low-skill jobs were increasingly exported to countries with surpluses of low-skill workers in peripheral regions of international capitalism, in the corporations' search for low wages and higher profits. Declining unionization rates ensued, and the labor movement triggered support of manufacturing protectionism as a way to shield the decreasing employment opportunities in unionized jobs in manufacturing.

In the 1980s, the agricultural peasant economy in Mexico experienced disinvestment, civil wars in Central America intensified, and growing inequality in the Caribbean and the rest of Latin America created a labor export system that functioned as a form of self-financed private insurance against unemployment, poverty, and civil war conflicts. In sum, in the last half century, millions of Latin American workers relocated temporarily or permanently to the United States, crossing multiple ethnic, class, cultural, colonial, and state borders. These crossings have reconfigured gender and family roles, community politics, civic engagements, ethnic identities, and survival strategies in the multiple locales these immigrants inhabit.[22]

MEXICAN AND CENTRAL AMERICAN IMMIGRATION

According to available official data, the Mexico–United States border is the largest migration corridor in the world. In 2014, more than 11.7 million Mexican immigrants resided in the United States, accounting for 28 percent of the 42.4 million foreign-born population—and by far the largest immigrant origin group in the country.[23] Today, there are more than 3 million Central Americans living in the United States, including a quarter of all Salvadorans. The vast majority of Central Americans arrived since the late 1970s, when social unrest and civil wars in their home countries encouraged large-scale migration.[24]

In terms of family remittances, Mexico was among the top ten receiving countries with the largest volume, obtaining $22.6 billion per year by 2010. As a percentage of national GDP, Honduras and El Salvador are among the top remittance receiving countries with 19 percent and 16 percent of their GDP being generated from family remittances, respectively. These monies have supported the social reproduction of millions of low-income households in Latin America. Mexico holds third place among the top ten remittance-receiving countries, following India and China.[25]

In an effort to protect the labor rights of its nationals who live in the United States and the vast remittances they send back to support millions of Mexican households, the Mexican government, taking advantage of its consular network in the United States, has created extensive partnerships with U.S. labor regulatory agencies, labor unions, workers' rights groups, and hometown associations (HTAs) to improve the well-being of Mexican workers who live abroad.[26] Facing a Republican presidency that threatened to deport all the undocumented, the lack of progress to achieve a congressional bipartisan agreement to fix the broken federal immigration system, and the June 23, 2016, announcement of the U.S. Supreme Court deadlock in a case challenging President Obama's immigration plan to regularize the status of millions of undocumented immigrants, the possibilities of social incorporation for many of these workers lies in the scarce services provided to them by their consular networks and civil society organizations. Undocumented workers pose a challenge to labor standards enforcement agencies and to those who advocate on their behalf. They are on the one hand precluded from legal employment and subject to deportability, but on the other hand they enjoy a range of workplace rights in arenas ranging from wage and hours to discrimination and workplace safety.[27]

In the United States, according to the Organization for Economic Co-Operation and Development (OECD), 25.3 percent of workers face "low pay"—earning less than two-thirds of the median wage. In fact, low-wage workers fare worse in the United States than any other OECD nation.[28] In the future, millions of new jobs will be created by low-wage industries, many of which will likely employ immigrants, including in-home health care aides for the retiring baby boomers, restaurant employees, warehouse services, and domestic workers. A large number of immigrants from Latin America and other countries generally arrive with low levels of formal education compared to U.S. norms, so they often end up in low-wage jobs.[29] A sizable proportion of these immigrants lack legal status, and the children growing up in homes where parents lack legal status have been shown to be disadvantaged even when they themselves have been born in the United States and are therefore citizens.[30]

However, it is important to note that the profile of many of these migrants has changed in recent years and new trends may emerge. Between 2006 and 2012, Mexico showed the most important growth among Latin American and Caribbean nations in its share of migrants with a university degree living in the United States, going from 440,000 to 593,000 qualified Mexican migrants, representing a 35 percent increase in that six-year period.[31]

UNDOCUMENTED MIGRATION TRENDS

Despite the persistent weight of Mexican immigrants as a percentage of the total foreign-born, Mexican unauthorized immigration rates are decreasing. As Ana González-Barrera and Jens M. Krogstad from the Pew Research Center explain in their 2015 calculations, "the number of Mexican immigrants living in the U.S. illegally has declined. In 2014, 5.6 million unauthorized immigrants from Mexico live in the U.S., down by about 1 million since 2007. Despite the drop, Mexicans still make up about half (49% in 2014) of unauthorized immigrants."[32] Mexican demographers find that Mexican municipalities with the highest levels of insecurity are less likely to migrate both to the United States and even internally, due in part to the violence produced by the war against drugs.[33]

Despite negative portrayals in the media as a burden to local economies, undocumented workers pay federal, state, and local taxes, including personal income taxes, property taxes, Social Security, and sales or excise taxes, collectively paying an estimated $11.64 billion a year, according to the Institute on Taxation and Economic Policy. Contributions range from almost $2.2 million in Montana with an estimated undocumented population of 4,000 to more than $3.1 billion in California, home to more than 3 million undocumented immigrants. If granted legal status under comprehensive immigration reform, they would be paying $2.1 billion more in taxes.[34] In a 2010 briefing before the United States Commission on Civil Rights, held in Washington, DC, a panel of economists agreed that "illegal immigration to the United States in recent decades has tended to depress both wages and employment rates for low-skilled American citizens," although the panelists couldn't agree on whether the effect was "modest" or "significant."[35]

New survey research on undocumented migration to the United States by sociology and law professor Emily Ryo shows that perceptions of availability of Mexican jobs and the dangers of border crossing are significant determinants of the intentions to migrate without documents, whereas certainty of apprehension and the severity of punishment are not significant determinants of the intent to migrate illegally. These findings suggest the significance of procedural justice and fairness perceptions. Due to the moral ambiguity that frequently characterizes immigration law, social and institutional tensions exist to decide the kind of policy that is appropriate when it comes to unauthorized migration. As Ryo explains, "to many would-be migrants, as well as U.S. citizens, there is a lack of moral credibility to a law perceived as preventing individuals from working to support their families. For many, there is also no moral credibility to a law that seems to punish individuals for satisfying the demands of U.S. households and corporations for cheap foreign labor."[36]

The decline of Mexican migration to the United States is also correlated to multiple well-identified factors: changes in the demographic profile including lower fertility rates, decreased circularity after heightened enforcement, higher levels of education, dramatic increases in the costs of crossing, higher unemployment paired with slower demographic growth in the border region, the Great Recession that began in 2007, and decreased family remittances to finance new migrations.[37] Besides, tenure insecurity and restrictions on land markets (especially rentals) are still important barriers to migration both internally and internationally, especially in rural areas.[38]

The eight-year Obama administration returned or removed a record 2.4 million immigrants using fairly punitive measures. As deportation historian Adam Goodman explains, "removal comes with an automatic five- or 10-year ban on applying to re-enter the country; if apprehended a second time, migrants could face incarceration and a 20-year or lifetime ban from re-entry."[39] The increase in deportations during the Obama years was largely a consequence of the Illegal Immigration Reform and Immigrant Responsibility Act (IIRIRA), signed by former president Bill Clinton in 1996. This law expanded the number of deportable offenses, called for the mandatory detention and removal of legal permanent residents convicted of aggravated felonies, limited discretionary relief from deportation, and established bars on returning to the United States after being in the country without authorization. Between 2004 and 2013, more than 2.4 million Mexicans migrants without legal authorization were deported to Mexico.[40] In an attempt to call national attention to the disturbing consequences of family separations due to deportations, several grassroots movements across the United States have emerged with a single policy objective—legalization for unauthorized immigrants—and a single tactic—halting deportations through employing civil disobedience, with some modest results.[41]

The deterrence effects of the massive deportations during the Obama administration effectively quadrupled the number of returned migrants to Mexico with significant U.S. labor experience between 2007 and 2012. This number now reaches 1 million. From 2006 to 2016, the population born in the United States but living in Mexico doubled, so that there are 773,000 people living in Mexico who were born in the United States by 2016. Yet, the decline in migration from Mexico has been followed by an increase of Central Americans fleeing violence and attempting to enter the United States as refugees. From 2011 to 2016, the U.S. government requested aid from the Mexican government to jointly deport 800,000 refugees to Central America, including 40,000 children. These families with young children are being forced to return to deteriorating conditions of violence. Drug mafias and criminal gangs drove them out of Guatemala, Honduras, and El Salvador, where they will likely be targeted on their return.[42]

By and large, the increase in deportations has not produced the desired deterrence effects in the targeted region. According to Marc Rosenblum, deputy director of the Migration Policy Institute's U.S. Immigration Policy Program, "between 2011 and 2014, the number of Central American unaccompanied children (UACs) and 'family units'—parents traveling with young children—who arrived at the U.S.-Mexico border increased rapidly, reaching a peak of 137,000 in fiscal year 2014."[43] This massive emigration of UACs from Central America is attributed to a combination of crime and violence affecting youths in the region, economic concerns, poor educational systems, and a desire to reconnect with family members.

TEMPORARY WORK VISAS

Regardless of visa category, employment sector, race, gender, or national origin, internationally recruited workers face disturbingly common patterns of recruitment abuse, including fraud, discrimination, severe economic coercion, retaliation, blacklisting, and, in some cases, forced labor, indentured servitude, debt bondage, and human trafficking. Many temporary work visas lack the necessary government oversight to ensure that employers comply with state and federal labor laws.[44]

Up until the end of 2016, in addition to the roughly 56,000 temporary agricultural workers admitted through the H-2A program, the United States was admitting more than a half-million international workers each year to perform jobs across an increasingly wide range of employment sectors.[45] Internationally recruited workers are employed as landscapers, domestic workers, carnival workers, forestry workers, seafood workers, hotel workers, maids, janitors, herders, computer programmers, engineers, nurses, and public school teachers.

One of the temporary visa programs that attracted attention and criticism in recent years is the H-1B visa program. Capped by Congress in 2014 at 85,000 annual visas per year, this program was created by the Immigration Act of 1990. Reserved for those in "specialty occupations" requiring at least a bachelor's degree, the H-1B has become a useful recruitment tool to bring engineers for the information technology sector but also is used to bring doctors, teachers, scientists, and university professors.[46] Recent journalistic reports have documented how large outsourcing and recruitment companies have gamed the system. Nowadays, a mere thirteen outsourcing companies based in India capture one-third of the H-1B visas, frequently paying below market rate for comparable occupations in the U.S. labor market.[47] In 2016, a small group of technology workers who had been displaced by H-1B visa holders brought lawsuits in federal courts against Disney World in Florida, Abbot Laboratories in Illinois, and two global consulting companies, HCL and Cognizant. According to Professor Hal Salzman, a labor force expert at Rutgers University, global consulting and recruitment companies have taken advantage of loopholes in the temporary visa rules.[48] As a consequence, tens of thousands of U.S. workers were replaced by foreign workers holding H-1B and other temporary visas in the five years from 2011 to 2016.

Yet, the United States is highly dependent on recruited labor in agriculture, a critical sector of the economy that has helped to maintain reasonable low prices for fresh produce available to the middle class. Between 1989 and 2009, the share of undocumented immigrants doing farmwork rose from less than 10 percent to about half the agricultural labor force; guest workers under the H-2A visa program make up a much smaller share.[49] This is an economic sector with scarce opportunities for upward social mobility. According to a 2014 study commissioned by the Chicago Council of Global affairs, there's a severe employment shortage in the agricultural sector: "Over the last century, roughly three million migrant and seasonal farmworkers, on average, were in the U.S. at any one time. But as of 2012 that number had dropped to 1.06 million, including part-time and full-time workers, according to the Farm Labor Survey conducted by the US Department of Agriculture's (USDA) National Agricultural Statistics Service."[50] In the Midwest, there are 57,000 legal immigrants with work visas in agriculture, livestock raising, and food processing; however, this sector needs another 80,000 workers immediately. Indeed, half of the 440 U.S. counties that depend on agriculture are located in the Midwest.[51] This imported labor force is needed due to the identification of farm labor in the United States as an "immigrant job category" over the last few decades, which created a stigmatization of that type of work among native-born Americans, making it unattractive to many even as an employment opportunity of last resort.[52]

Filling up agricultural positions, both temporary and year-round will require innovation in the agricultural industry as labor shortages are predicted to continue. Economists Edward Taylor, Diane Charlton, and Antonio Yúñez-Naude have analyzed panel data from rural Mexico, and their evidence suggests that the same shift from farmwork that characterized U.S. labor history is well underway in Mexico. In the future, U.S. agriculture will compete with Mexican farms for a dwindling supply of farm labor. According to these economists, "since U.S. domestic workers are unwilling to do farm work and the United States can feasibly import farm workers from only a few countries in close geographic proximity, the agricultural industry will eventually need to adjust production to use less labor."[53] Meanwhile, the tightly regulated contract-worker migration among contracted (H-2A) agricultural workers in the United States forces many parents to leave their children for seven months of the year. In other cases, migrant parents are unable to bring their children because the parents are undocumented. Each year, thousands of migrants have to accept these restrictive contracts that provide a higher salary while effectively preventing family reunification or regular travel since those contracts do not lead to legal permanent settlement. The United States has yet to find efficient ways to attract the low-wage workers that the economy needs without having to import thousands of them from abroad. Without effective solutions, immigrants with and without papers will continue to take low-paid and exploitive jobs because few citizens are willing to accept the low-wage and poorly regulated conditions of those industries.

SOCIAL INCLUSION

Many residents in metropolitan regions across the United States now recognize the positive impact immigrants have made in the economic revitalization of their communities. They acknowledge the reliability of the immigrant workforce and the ways in which immigrants contribute to local economies by establishing households, starting small businesses, and paying taxes. Some employers express a preference for immigrant workers, whether because of the lower wages they often demand or because they are a more pliable workforce than native-born workers. Due to the undocumented status of millions of low-wage immigrant workers and the failure of workplace protections in the United States, many immigrant workers are still vulnerable to exploitation, the violation of their civil and labor rights, and the threat of deportation.[54] Therefore, collective efforts to increase the possibilities of social integration are crucial to improve their chances of social mobility. Besides the opportunities to carve unique social spaces in cities and neighborhoods, full social inclusion of immigrant communities implies recognition as a legitimate part of the national community, parity of critical life chances, including the right to obtain a postsecondary credential or raise one's children in a racially integrated neighborhood with good schools and safe streets.[55]

To achieve successful social integration outcomes, state and city governments with large immigrant populations need to understand the benefits of full incorporation. With Republican elected officials frequently leaning in anti-immigrant directions and increased income polarization facilitating scapegoating of minorities, the challenge of integrating immigrants can often involve coalitions of odd bedfellows. Therefore, it is important to incorporate businesses and labor groups as important allies in discussions for immigrant integration and understand why these two groups are more likely to end up in the pro-immigrant side rather than the anti-immigrant side. Immigrant incorporation is key to reduce the negative impacts that increases in the share of immigrants might have such as the growth of low-wage labor, poorly regulated suburban development, and declining labor standards. Observing how metropolitan leaders manage the mix of costs and benefits is important for immigrant integration but also to improve regional governance and re-silience.[56]

Local leaders need to have access to best practices that might offer good opportunities for replication. For example, using demographic and violence information at the neighborhood level for a representative sample of eighty-seven large cities, a recent study reveals that favorable immigrant political opportunities reduce violent crime in neighborhoods with high concentrations of immigrants. Researchers speculate that this positive relationship happens because "favorable political contexts bolster social organization by enhancing trust and public social control within immigrant neighborhoods."[57]

The individual trajectories of specific places in the realm of immigrant incorporation and national political debates also influence the degree of local receptivity. Areas that had already developed substantial immigrant communities by the mid-1980s benefited from Republican president Ronald Reagan's support for integrating the undocumented. Right after the Immigration Reform and Control Act (IRCA) of 1986, large metropolitan areas benefited from a $4 billion investment in federal funds to support immigrant paths to legalization and full inclusion via naturalizations.[58] Since then, no other similar federal effort has been undertaken to incorporate immigrants and few state governments have tried to fill the gap. With the exception of modest federal spending on adult education, the integration-related costs of civic education, cross-cultural communication, learning English, and legal aid have been borne either by the immigrants themselves or by private institutions and local governments. As Janet Murguía and Cecilia Muñoz put it, "Perhaps the most extraordinary thing about the integration of immigrants in this nation of immigrants is just how much it is being done by the immigrants themselves, with a minimum of effort by government or society at large. Despite widespread hand-wringing that today's immigrants are not learning English or becoming 'like us' as they used to, the traditional indicators—English-language acquisition, workforce participation, homeownership, military service, civic participation, and intermarriage—make it clear that immigrants continue to do what they have always done: become Americans relatively quickly. We're getting an enormous return on a tiny investment."[59] Considering the scant public investment for immigrant integration, it is not surprising that naturalization rates vary greatly state by state even for the same national groups because the civic organization landscape looks very different in Phoenix, which is in the anti-immigrant state of Arizona; compared to that of Chicago, in the more pro-immigrant state of Illinois. Past research indicates that the naturalization rates, at least among Mexican legal permanent residents vary by a factor of two, both across and within states.

Notwithstanding the small public investments in immigrant integration, there are some examples that point towards best practices. In 2008, the National League of Cities (NLC), a coalition representing 19,000 cities across the nation, launched the Municipal Action for Immigrant Integration (MAII), a program aimed at assisting local officials in managing the challenges posed by immigrant integration. The two main components of the program are city-level naturalization campaigns and citizenship community initiatives to help local officials develop tailored action plans for immigrant integration. As journalist James Fallows discovered in his 52,000-mile journey around the United States in a single-engine plane, one of the eleven characteristics that can predict the future success of cities is that they make themselves open, trying to attract and include new people, including foreigners and refugees.[60]

Since its inception, MAII has successfully implemented twenty initiatives that showcase best practices for immigrant integration. These twenty cities are very diverse, ranging in size from large to small, and from varying geographic locations. The practices are good examples of public and private partnerships, advisory initiatives, and action-oriented programs. Many of the cities have multiple programs addressing multiple issues, while others focus on one specific issue or topic. They represent a wide variety of states, including places with long-standing immigrant populations such as New York City and Los Angeles, as well as newer emerging destinations in the South, including Chattanooga, Tennessee, and Durham, North Carolina.

Taken together, these twenty city-level programs recognize the challenges and opportunities posed by immigrant incorporation and issue several recommendations to improve immigrant incorporation outcomes across cities facing challenges to incorporate diverse immigrant populations. Some of those are worth highlighting:

1. Local governments should play a role in the development of a nationwide strategy for immigrant integration.

2. Partnerships with state governments should be strengthened, and the relationship between state and local law enforcement agencies needs to be clear.

3. Engagement with civil society organizations in the host community, including immigrant-organizations, faith-based organizations, and the business sector, should be encouraged.

4. Mayoral advisory boards and immigrant affairs offices should be established.

5. Elimination of language barriers and promotion of adult literacy should be encouraged to eliminate significant obstacles in the life of immigrant residents.[61]

To illustrate the important role that state and local governments should play in immigrant incorporation, we can look at the experience of Illinois, which is a good example of virtuous circles between public-private partnerships and robust immigrant-led grassroots organizations. In 2005, Illinois enacted the New Americans Initiative, a bipartisan initiative aimed at facilitating immigrant integration. The initiative encouraged citizenship acquisition among eligible permanent residents, provided funds for English-language instruction, and established an Office of New Americans to coordinate policies, actions, planning, and programs of the state government with respect to immigrant integration and the impact of national immigration policies.[62]

The nationally recognized public-private partnership established through the New Americans Initiative led to the creation of Illinois Welcoming Centers, government-supported institutions that have assisted over 50,000 immigrants in attaining citizenship and thousands more in gaining access to services and benefits. Through its multiethnic advisory board, the City of Chicago's Office of New Americans (ONA), has been able to address language access through a new city ordinance and create greater accessibility to city programs and resources. In 2012, ONA set the goal of helping ten thousand immigrants to become U.S. citizens in three years by encouraging them to independently initiate their naturalization process. In partnership with the Illinois Coalition of Immigrant and Refugee Rights and the U.S. Citizenship and Immigration Services (USCIS), 58,160 immigrants became naturalized citizens in the 2005–12 period. To support the full incorporation of immigrants, ONA also hosts the New Americans Small Business Series, a quarterly event that fosters small business growth in immigrant communities throughout Chicago.[63] The same year, Mayor Rahm Emanuel introduced a Welcoming City Ordinance incorporating basic protections for undocumented Chicagoans who have not been convicted of a serious crime and are not wanted on a criminal warrant.

The city of San Jose, California, lies within Santa Clara County, an area with large immigrant populations and a county government that has become a significant pro-immigrant actor. San Jose itself has innovative policies to integrate immigrants, including a cultural proficiency initiative initiated by the Santa Clara County Office of Human Relations. Since 1996, the county has offered immigrant integration services in the city, including free citizenship days, educational programs, and a cultural proficiency initiative. In 2008, a free citizenship day was offered in nine languages, including Spanish. The Santa Clara County Office of Human Relations began offering a loan program using funds from local private foundations to cover the citizenship application costs for eligible low-income permanent residents after the office observed a drop in applications when naturalization fees increased.[64]

While these accomplishments are important to highlight, continuation of these initiatives is highly dependent on financial support from public funds. Continued access to public funds to finance immigrant integration is in peril amid current budgetary concerns for the City of Chicago and the State of Illinois, but considering the enormous social and economic benefits that naturalization brings to immigrant communities, funding for these programs should be a priority.

CITIZENSHIP TRENDS

While immigrants have varying motivations regarding the citizenship process, access to supportive institutions may be a key factor allowing those who are motivated to move forward. Nevertheless, national origin is the most common key variable used to explain citizenship acquisition among those eligible. Surprisingly, there is no consensus among pro-immigrant and anti-immigrant advocates on the importance of encouraging full citizenship for those already eligible. Reading national statistics on naturalization of legal permanent residents, a casual observer might conclude that this is a loyalty competition determined by national origin and "national political culture", a highly voluntaristic model of naturalization decision making that does not account for the role of institutional barriers.

As political scientists Jonathan Fox explains,

> the conventional approach to analyzing variation in naturalization patterns focuses on differences across national origin. This approach suggests that

differences in national political cultures are a key factor in explaining naturalization decisions. While citizenship decisions certainly are influenced by
the political cultures that immigrants bring with them, their perception of
access to the citizenship process may also be strongly influenced by their level
of formal education. Indeed, the citizenship exam is a de facto literacy test.
Command of the English language is also relevant, which in turn is influenced
by social class and access to quality language instruction. Access to reliable
legal support is also crucial for immigrants to trust that they can navigate
the process successfully. Indeed, researchers know remarkably little about
what factors determine applicant success rates. While there is official data on
success rates in the citizenship test, these figures underestimate the overall
non-completion rate, which is likely to be substantially higher.[65]

Observing differences in institutional barriers at the local level helps explain
state variations in citizenship rates even among the same national origin
groups. Context matters to determine the availability of resources needed to
promote naturalization at the state and county levels. Promoting citizenship
among legal permanent residents contributes to the economic and cultural
vitality of cities and increases global competitiveness. Compared to nonciti-
zen immigrants, naturalized immigrants have incomes that are 14.6 percent
higher, and poverty rates that are 9.9 percent lower.[66] Increasing the numbers
of naturalized citizens helps expands the tax base and reduces reliance on
city services. Citizenship also increases the quality of U.S. democratic life
by enfranchising thousands of residents to vote in local, state, and national
elections. In addition to the right to vote, naturalized immigrants are eligible
to participate in federal programs, gain a number of legal rights, and become
eligible for federal employment.

According to Pew Hispanic Center estimates (now Pew Research Center's
Hispanic Trends Project), the share of all legal foreign-born residents who
became naturalized U.S. citizens rose to 56 percent in 2011, representing the
highest level in three decades and an increase of 18 percentage points since
1990. The population of naturalized U.S. citizens reached 15.5 million in 2011.
While Latin Americans historically had lower rates of naturalization than
immigrants from other regions, for reasons that are still not well understood,
their numbers have increased sharply. For example, Proposition 187 in California, Mexico's dual nationality law of 1996, and the tightening of the immigration laws in 1996 encouraged many to become citizens. Mexico's official
recognition of the legitimacy of dual nationality has made U.S. citizenship
more attractive to those immigrants who want eventually to return.[67]

As of 2011, 9.7 million immigrants were eligible for naturalization but had not yet naturalized; of these, more than a third were Mexican immigrants. Compared with other immigrants from Latin America and the Caribbean, Mexicans still have the lowest rate of naturalization—36 percent versus 61 percent in 2011. In July 2007, USCIS nearly doubled the fee for naturalization processing and added a biometric fee. The new cost has effectively shut off access to naturalization for low-wage immigrant workers, as has the limited availability of loans from private institutions.

While the numbers of new citizens have been growing faster than the numbers of new permanent residents, a huge backlog of eligible immigrants persists. Nationwide, in the five months prior to January 2016, average requests for citizenship reached 65,000 per month, with half the applicants being Latino. In a regular year, some 650,000 green-card holders are granted citizenship. In the 2016 electoral year, due in large part to the anti-immigrant narrative that the GOP orchestrated against Latino immigrants,[68] a number of Latino-led organizations set the goal of naturalizing eligible Latino immigrant in higher numbers. In the words of Rocío Sáenz, a national leader of the Service Employees International Union, "there is a sense of urgency as a result of the hateful rhetoric about mass deportations, building walls, calling us criminals—this is personal for us."[69] Sáenz, a Mexican immigrant and a veteran of the Justice for Janitors Campaign, is part of a coalition that has helped 12,781 Latinos apply for citizenship in more than three hundred "naturalization workshops" around the country. The triumph of Democratic candidate Hillary Clinton in the state of Nevada both in the Democratic primaries and in the general election was supported by the nascent power of the Latino electorate in the metropolitan areas of Las Vegas and Reno.

The evidence presented here suggests the need for a broad reassessment of the determinants of citizenship decisions and the availability of programs aimed at encouraging citizenship. Those interested in promoting citizenship among permanent residents could use new research tools that could address not only motivations but also perceived barriers in the naturalization process. Available evidence suggests that the context within which immigrants make naturalization decisions matters. The prospects for closing the gap between eligible legal residents and new citizens depends heavily on whether or not the federal government makes immigrant integration a policy priority. New immigrant minorities who have played by the rules need to have access to the same opportunities afforded to other immigrant and ethnic minorities in the past. For immigrant social inclusion to succeed, it is necessary to increase the opportunities for immigrants and their descendants to obtain equal opportunities in a society, as well as social acceptance, through participation in major institutions such as the educational and political system and the labor and housing markets without discrimination. More contact and interaction is needed between immigrants and the native-born population to achieve a better understanding of each other.

Notes

1. "America's Foreign Born in the Last 50 Years," How Do We Know?, United States Census Bureau, 2010, accessed April 25, 2017, www.census.gov/content/dam/Census/library/visualizations/2013/comm/foreign_born_text.pdf.

2. "Modern Immigration Wave Brings 59 Million to U.S., Driving Population Growth and Change through 2065: Views of Immigration's Impact on U.S. Society Mixed," Hispanic Trends, Pew Research Center, September 28, 2015, accessed April 25 2017, www.pewhispanic.org.

3. Jeffrey S. Passel, D'Vera Cohn, and Mark Hugo López, "Hispanics Account for More than Half of Nation's Growth in Past Decade," Hispanic Trends, Pew Research Center, March 24, 2011, accessed April 25, 2017, www.pewhispanic.org.

4. On the raid mentality, see John Tirman, *Dream Chasers: Immigration and the American Backlash* (Boston: MIT Press, 2015).

5. Andrew K. Sandoval Strausz, "Latino Landscapes: Postwar Cities and the Transnational Origins of a New Urban America," *Journal of American History* 101, no. 3 (2014): 804–31, doi:10.1093/jahist/jau657.

6. Isabel Wilkerson, *The Warmth of Other Suns: The Epic Story of America's Great Migration* (New York: Vintage Books, 2010), location 275 Kindle edition.

7. Ibid., location 309, Kindle edition.

8. Richard Alba and Nancy Foner, "Integration's Challenges and Opportunities in the Wealthy West," *Journal of Ethnic and Migration Studies* 42, no. 1 (2016): 3–22, doi:10.1080/1369183X.2015.1083770.

9. Richard Alba and Victor Nee, *Remaking the American Mainstream: Assimilation and Contemporary Immigration* (Cambridge, MA: Harvard University Press, 2013).

10. "Modern Immigration Wave."

11. Fernando Lozano Asencio, Luciana Gandini, and Ana Elizabeth Jardón Hernández, *Condiciones laborales en tiempos de crisis. Un análisis de la migración calificada de América Latina y el Caribe en Estados Unidos* (México, DF: Universidad Nacional Autónoma de México, 2015), 31.

12. The EB-5 visa program is available to migrants who can invest a minimum of $500,000 for the creation of at least ten new jobs in economically distressed places or a minimum of $1 million for the creation of these jobs outside of such areas.

13. Rogelio Sáenz, "A Transformation in Mexican Migration to the United States," *Carsey Research*, National Issue Brief no. 86, summer 2015.

14. Cybelle Fox, *Three Worlds of Relief: Race, Immigration, and the American Welfare State from the Progressive Era to the New Deal* (Princeton, NJ: Princeton University Press, 2012).

15. John Bodnar, "Ethnic Fraternal Benefit Associations: Their Historical Development, Character and Significance," in *Records of Ethnic Fraternal Benefit Associations in the United States: Essays and Inventories* (St. Paul, MN: Immigration History Research Center, 1981), 5–14. John Bodnar, *The Transplanted: A History of Immigrants in Urban America* (Bloomington: Indiana University Press, 1985).

16. Xóchitl Bada, *Mexican Hometown Associations in Chicagoacán: From Local to Transnational Civic Engagement* (New Brunswick, NJ: Rutgers University Press 2014).

17. Douglas S. Massey, Jorge Durand, and Nolan J. Malone, *Beyond Smoke and Mirrors. Mexican Immigration in an Era of Economic Integration* (New York: Russell Sage Foundation, 2002). Mae M. Ngai, *Impossible Subjects: Illegal Aliens and the Making of Modern America* (Princeton, NJ: Princeton University Press, 2004). Aristide R. Zolberg, *A Nation by Design: Immigration Policy in the Fashioning of America* (New York: Russell Sage Foundation, 2006).

18. Guillermo J. Grenier and Lisandro Pérez, *The Legacy of Exile: Cubans in the United States* (Boston: Allyn and Bacon, 2003). Peggy Levitt, *The Transnational Villagers* (Berkeley: University of California Press, 2001). Cecilia Menjívar, *Fragmented Ties: Salvadoran Immigrant Networks in America* (Berkeley: University of California Press, 2000).

19. Jonathan Fox and Libby Haight, *Subsidizing Inequality: Mexican Corn Policy since NAFTA* (Washington, DC: Woodrow Wilson International Center for Scholars / University of California, Santa Cruz, 2011).

20. Import-substitution industrialization (ISI) is an economic model implemented by Latin American nations, which aims at reducing economic dependency from foreign capitals. Many external and internal factors led to the demise of this model. Among them was its inability to absorb migrant labor in urban areas and the increase in urban poverty. Also, the agricultural sector was stagnant, increasing inflation and making it impossible to attain self-sufficiency. After World War II, ISI became a deliberate policy tool for economic development. According to Werner Baer, "the principal policy instruments used to promote and intensify ISI in Latin America were: protective tariffs and/or exchange controls; special preferences for domestic and foreign firms importing capital goods for new industries; preferential import exchange rates for industrial raw materials, fuels and intermediate goods; cheap loans by government development banks for favored industries; the construction by governments of infrastructure specially designed to complement industries; and the direct participation of government in certain industries, especially the heavier industries, such as steel, where neither domestic nor foreign private capital was willing or able to invest." Werner Baer, "Import Substitution and Industrialization in Latin America: Experiences and Interpretations," *Latin America Research Review* 7 (1972): 95–122, accessed April 25, 2017, www.jstor.org/stable/2502457.

21. Baer, "Import Substitution and Industrialization," Frank Bonilla, Edwin Meléndez, Rebecca Morales, and María de los Angeles Torres, eds., *Borderless Borders: U.S. Latinos, Latin Americans, and the Paradox of Interdependence* (Philadelphia: Temple University Press, 1998).

22. Adriana Cruz-Manjarrez, *Zapotecs on the Move: Cultural, Social, and Political Processes in Transnational Perspective* (New Brunswick, NJ: Rutgers University Press, 2013). Lynn Stephen, *Transborder Lives: Indigenous Oaxacans in Mexico, California, and Oregon* (Durham, NC: Duke University Press, 2007).

23. Jie Zong and Jeanne Batalova, "Mexican Immigrants in the United States," *Spotlight, the Online Journal of the Migration Policy Institute*, March 17, 2016.

24. Norma Stoltz Chinchilla and Nora Hamilton, "Central America," in *The New Americans: A Guide to Immigration since 1965*, ed. Mary C. Waters and Reed Ueda, 328–39 (Cambridge, MA: Harvard University Press, 2007).

25. World Bank, *Migration and Remittances Factbook* (Washington, DC: World Bank, 2011).

26. Xóchitl Bada and Shannon Gleeson, "A New Approach to Migrant Labor Rights Enforcement: The Crisis of Undocumented Worker Abuse and Mexican Consular Advocacy in the United States," *Labor Studies Journal* 40 (2014): 32–53, doi:10.1177/0160449X14565112. Alexandra Délano, "The Diffusion of Diaspora Engagement Policies: A Latin American Agenda," *Political Geography* 41 (2013): 90–100, doi:10.1016/j.polgeo.2013.11.007.

27. To learn more about the precarious status of undocumented workers, see Shannon Gleeson, *Precarious Claims: The Promise and Failure of Workplace Protections in the United States* (Oakland: University of California Press, 2016)

28. Lawrence Mishel, "The United States Leads in Low-Wage Work and the Lowest Wages for Low-Wage Workers," Working Economics Blog, Economic Policy Institute, September 4, 2014, accessed April 25, 2017, www.epi.org.

29. Roger Waldinger and Michael Lichter, *How the Other Half Works: Immigration and the Social Organization of Labor* (Berkeley: University of California, 2003).

30. Frank Bean, Mark A. Leach, Susan K. Brown, James D. Bachmeier, and John R. Hipp, "The Educational Legacy of Unauthorized Immigration: Comparisons across US-Immigrant Groups in How Parents' Status Affects Their Offspring," *International Migration Review* 45 (2011): 348–85. Hirokazu Yoshikawa, *Immigrants Raising Citizens: Undocumented Parents and their Young Children* (New York: Russell Sage Foundation, 2011).

31. Asencio, Gandini, and Jardón Hernández, *Condiciones laborales*, 37.

32. Ana González-Barrera and Jens Manuel Krogstad, "What We Know about Illegal Immigration from Mexico," Pew Research Center, November 20, 2015.

33. Agustín Escobar Latapí, "La migración México–Estados Unidos–México. Más allá de lo laboral," working paper presented to the Katz Center for Mexican Studies, University of Chicago, April 19, 2016.

34. Lisa Christensen Gee, Matthew Gardner, and Meg Wiehe, "Undocumented Immigrants' State and Local Tax Contributions," Institute on Taxation and Economic Policy, February 2016, accessed April 25, 2017, www.itep.org.

35. "The Impact of Illegal Immigration on the Wages and Employment Opportunities of Black Workers," briefing report, United States Commission on Civil Rights,

2010, accessed August 1, 2016, http://digitalcommons.ilr.cornell.edu/cgi/viewcontent .cgi?article=1756&context=key_workplace.

36. Emily Ryo, "Deciding to Cross: Norms and Economics of Unauthorized Migration," *American Sociological Review* 78, no. 4 (2013): 574–603, 594.

37. Damien Cave, "Better Lives for Mexicans Cut Allure of Going North," *New York Times*, July 6, 2011, accessed April 25, 2017, www.nytimes.com.

38. Alain De Janvry, Kyle Emerick, Marco Gonzalez-Navarro, and Elisabeth Sadoulet, *Delinking Land Rights from Land Use: Certification and Migration in Mexico*, August 11, 2014, accessed April 25, 2017, www.ocf.berkeley.edu/~kemerick/certification _and_migration.pdf.

39. Adam Goodman, "How the Deportation Numbers Mislead," Opinion, Aljazeera America, January 24, 2014, accessed April 25, 2017, http://america.aljazeera.com.

40. "Table 41. Aliens Removed by Criminal Status and Region and Country of Nationality: Fiscal Years 2004 to 2013," in *2013 Yearbook of Immigration Statistics* Office of Immigration Statistics, U.S. Department of Homeland Security, 107–15, accessed April 25, 2017, www.dhs.gov/sites/default/files/publications/ois_yb_2013_0.pdf.

41. Amalia Pallares, *Family Activism: Immigrant Struggles and the Politics of Noncitizenship* (New Brunswick, NJ: Rutgers University Press, 2014).

42. Nicholas Kristoff, "We're Helping Deport Kids to Die," *New York Times*, July 16, 2016.

43. Marc R. Rosenblum, "Unaccompanied Child Migration to the United States: The Tension between Protection and Prevention," Migration Policy Institute Report, April 2015, 2, accessed April 25, 2017, www.migrationpolicy.org.

44. International Labor Recruitment Working Group, *The American Dream Up for Sale: A Blueprint for Ending International Labor Recruitment Abuse*, February 2013.

45. The H-2A work visa allows a foreign national entry into the United States for temporary or seasonal agricultural work.

46. Jeanne Batalova, "H-1B Temporary Skilled Worker Program," *Spotlight*, Migration Policy Institute, October 7, 2010.

47. Haeyoun Park, "How Outsourcing Companies Are Gaming the Visa System," *New York Times*, November 10, 2015. Julia Preston, "Large Companies Game H-1B Visa Program, Costing the U.S. Jobs," *New York Times*, November 10, 2015.

48. Cited in Preston, "Large Companies."

49. Eduardo Porter, "Competing Views on How to Regulate Illegal Migration," *New York Times*, October 30, 2016, accessed April 25, 2017, www.nytimes.com. Eduardo Porter, "Laid-Off Americans, Required to Zip Lips on Way Out, Grow Bolder," *New York Times*, June 11, 2016.

50. Stephanie Mercier, *Employing Agriculture: How the Midwest Farm and Food Sector Relies on Immigrant Labor*, Chicago Council on Global Affairs Immigration Initiative, December 2014, 3.

51. Ibid.

52. Elizabeth Dwoskin, "Why Americans Won't Do Dirty Jobs," *Bloomberg Businessweek*, November 9, 2011, accessed August 1, 2016,www.businessweek.com.

53. J. Edward Taylor, Diane Charlton, and Antonio Yúñez-Naude, "The End of Farm Labor Abundance," *Applied Economic Perspectives and Policy* 34, no. 4 (2012): 587–98, 587.

54. Shannon Gleeson, *Precarious Claims: The Promise and Failure of Workplace Protections in the United States* (Berkeley: University of California Press, 2016).

55. Alba and Foner, "Integration's Challenges."

56. Gleeson, *Precarious Claims*; John Mollenkopf and Manuel Pastor, eds., *Unsettled Americans: Metropolitan Context and Civic Leadership for Immigrant Integration* (Ithaca, NY: Cornell University Press, 2016).

57. Christopher J. Lyons, María B. Vélez, and Wayne A. Santoro, "Neighborhood Immigration, Violence, and City-Level Immigrant Political Opportunities," *American Sociological Review* 78, no. 4 (2013): 604–32, 604.

58. Doris Meissner, "Learning from History," *American Prospect*, October 23, 2005, accessed April 25, 2017, http://prospect.org.

59. Jonathan Fox, "Citizenship Trends: Growing Rates but Persistent Lags," in *Context Matters: Latino Immigrant Civic Engagement in Nine U.S. Cities*, by Xóchitl Bada, Jonathan Fox, Robert Donnelly, and Andrew Selee, "Reports on Latino Immigrant Civic Engagement, National Report," Woodrow Wilson International Center for Scholars, 2010, accessed April 25, 2017, www.wilsoncenter.org, 45.

60. James Fallows, "Eleven Signs a City Will Succeed," *Atlantic*, March 2016.

61. Ricardo Gambetta and Zivile Gedrimaite, *Municipal Innovations in Immigrant Integration: 20 Cities, 20 Good Practices*, Sustainable Cities Institute, National League of Cities, www.SustainableCitiesInstitute.org.

62. Bada et al., *Context Matters*.

63. "Mayor Emanuel Announces Chicago New Americans Initiative to Assist Eligible Immigrants Become U.S. Citizens," Mayor's Press Office, Chicago, June 12, 2012.

64. Bada et al., *Context Matters*; Mollenkopf and Pastor, *Unsettled Americans*.

65. Fox, "Citizenship Trends," 42.

66. "Mayor Emanuel Announces."

67. Ana González-Barrera, Mark Hugo López, Jeffrey S. Passel, and Paul Taylor, "The Path Not Taken: Two-Thirds of Legal Mexican Immigrants Are Not U.S. Citizens," Hispanic Trends, Pew Research Center, February 4, 2013, accessed April 25, 2017, www.pewhispanic.org.

68. *Republican Platform 2016*, accessed April 25, 2017, https://prod-static-ngop-pbl .s3.amazonaws.com/media/documents/DRAFT_12_FINAL[1]-ben_1468872234.pdf.

69. Richard Luscombe, Lauren Gambino, Dan Hernandez, and Ed Pilkington, "Will Latino Loathing of Trump Drive a Voter Movement to Swing the Election?," *Guardian*, U.S. edition, May 18, 2016, accessed April 25, 2017, www.theguardian.com.

Toward Reframing the Open Door

Policy, Pedagogy, and Developmental Education
in the Urban Community College

GREGORY V. LARNELL

TWYLA T. BLACKMOND LARNELL

JOHN BRAGELMAN

> The critical question is not who gains access to higher education,
> but rather what happens to people once they get there.
>
> —Jerome Karabel, "Community Colleges and Social Stratification"

Community colleges are positioned at a perpetual crossroads. By mission, these two-year postsecondary education institutions are intended primarily to broaden access to higher education credentialing; that is, their curricular and advisory offerings aim to facilitate transitions either to four-year university study or to career trajectories that may require a higher-skilled workforce than a traditional high-school education would satisfy. At the same time, community college admissions are open admissions or nonselective institutions, meaning that students are not denied admission based on entry tests or academic background.

Community colleges represent one-fourth of all higher educational institutions in the United States and serve nearly half of all undergraduates.[1] Furthermore, they serve "fully 58% of all African American undergraduates and 66% of all Hispanic undergraduates enrolled in community colleges." These institutions also welcome the working student—"more than half of 2-year college students are employed, compared to only 37% of 4-year college students."[2]

Although enrollments in two-year colleges rose briefly within the past decade—catalyzed by the most recent (U.S.) economic recession—completion rates have stagnated and have become a primary point of concern.[3]

Furthermore, for *urban* community colleges—those two-year institutions that draw the majority of their student population from their locations in or near metropolitan centers and, increasingly, from their satellite suburban communities—there is an added mission: urban community colleges have the conjoined goal of advancing individuals' social mobility and feeding the engines of corporate industrialism and commercialism.

In this latter sense, urban community colleges represent both a social resource for urban communities and a long-standing platform for fostering urban economic development. The emergence of a more service-based economy has increased the demand for labor with specialized knowledge, training, and skills. These new industries—particularly those that are more reliant on science, technology, engineering, and mathematics (STEM) fields—have elevated the importance of a postsecondary education, and mathematics continues to act as a primary gatekeeping discipline to STEM pathways.[4]

Developmental or remedial mathematics coursework, typically focused on the basic skills of arithmetic and algebra, has proven to be a mountainous obstacle for many students—disproportionately affecting those matriculating from inner-city public high schools or returning to college after being displaced from the labor market. Upon enrollment, however, a considerable number of these students are obligated to pass a remedial math course and often fail to progress to credit-bearing, "additive" courses.[5] Without these course credentials, students are less likely to complete their degree, which jeopardizes their economic future. To systematically counter this growing problem, policy making at the national and local levels has focused heavily on improving access to higher education in order to reduce economic inequalities and promote growth in the economy. Unfortunately, policy makers have failed to delve further into the complexity of "remediation," leaving many students stuck in place.

Toward shedding some light on this complexity and the distinctiveness of the community college structure, this chapter includes a broad curricular-disciplinary focus but also centers more directly on the particular context of developmental or remedial mathematics education. The primary purpose here is to explore several central components and tensions of urban community colleges and, specifically, how some of those components—policy, curriculum, administration, teaching, and learning—have been reframed since about 1980 to address market-driven concerns. We highlight how this convergence is reshaping teaching and learning in the urban community college and, particularly, how this convergence is conceptualized in policy, administered, implemented, and experienced.

PERSPECTIVES ON REMEDIATION AND REFORM

Originally referred to as junior colleges, two-year postsecondary institutions emerged in the late nineteenth century for the purpose of preparing high-school graduates for college by offering a general studies curriculum equivalent to the first two years of undergraduate study.[6] College and university administrators claimed that too many high-school graduates were not trained for the rigor of college courses, unable to finance tuition, or not prepared to reside on campuses away from home immediately after high school. The community college would then draw students from local neighborhoods and serve as a developmental and academic stepping-stone, offering services on life and study skills along with the traditional general education curricular offerings. Graduates would then earn a junior certificate (associate's degree in today's terms) and, if desired, could then transfer the junior certificate toward completing a baccalaureate degree. The convergence of high-school reforms and this fundamental restructuring of the postsecondary educational system ignited a persisting surge in high-school attendance and graduation and enrollments to junior colleges.

Although oriented toward broadening access, the development of junior colleges also functioned as a democratic-progressive tool that preserved the heightened statuses and differentiated missions of four-year universities. According to Josh Beach, junior colleges functioned systemically to "structurally limit opportunity to students in a hierarchically organized society."[7] The emergence of junior colleges gave rise to greater mission differentiation within the higher-education system and the social mobility functioning that it mediates. Junior colleges acted as a filter for traditional four-year colleges and universities by diverting certain groups, particularly low-income earners and persons of color, away from those institutions and potentially constraining their educational trajectories, thereby potentially limiting their economic futures. Reformers argued that the hierarchical system within higher education would encourage social efficiency by contributing to the creation of social classes according to race, gender, class, and religion.

Under the guise of college preparation, junior-college administration often emphasized vocational training for members of certain groups. The provision of *some* postsecondary education and professional training to those students facing increased discrimination would equip them to participate in the economy, but at lower levels. This would serve to support a social arrangement that could permanently relegate members of these groups to lower tiers of the socioeconomic ladder while allowing white and wealthy groups—economically stable or wealthy white men, in particular—to advance.

Emergence of the Community College

Despite the broader gatekeeping function of the junior college, the open-access mission of these institutions allowed many students to take advantage of the broadened array of educational opportunities. As these institutions grew and recruited generations of students throughout the twentieth century, the missions of these institutions expanded to address the changing economic and educational needs of the surrounding areas.[8] As this growth converged even more with U.S. political and economic interests (e.g., through the application of the GI Bill), the institutional potential of junior colleges gained even more momentum.

In times of economic crisis, the federal government has often called on junior colleges, specifically, to aid in filling the gap in the workforce by training individuals for mid- to low-skill industrial positions.[9] The Great Depression and World War II left many Americans unemployed and desperate for work. In the 1930s and 1940s, governmental leaders and administrators in higher education advocated for further expansion of vocational training at junior colleges. President Truman's Commission on Higher Education released a pivotal report that recommended national support for expanding access to "general education" by providing increased structural and budgetary support for the nation's growing number of junior colleges.[10]

Viewing the junior college experience as more of a terminal education rather than a college preparatory program, junior college administrators and faculty were encouraged to identify the demands of the hierarchically structured labor market and train the unemployed to fill the positions according to their diminished levels of professional training. In the 1960s, junior colleges experienced remarkable increases in student enrollment as veterans and baby boomers sought out semiprofessional training and minorities enrolled at higher rates. The Truman Commission argued that inequities in higher education, especially in access, had a negative effect on the economy by leaving many unprepared for the labor market. The commission did not specifically recommend that minorities and immigrants have access to the same higher-education opportunities; rather, the report emphasized a postsecondary education commensurate to their capabilities.[11] A lasting hallmark of the Truman Commission's report, however, was a rhetorical recommendation that junior colleges be re-termed "community colleges" in order to signal their strong institutional commitment to support members of their shared communities.

Current Challenges, National Trends, and Possibilities

The most recent, "great" recession of the mid-2000s ignited a historically significant shift in the U.S. economy, provoking sweeping structural changes in an already-shifting labor market. Moreover, a prior midcentury emphasis on domestic industrial manufacturing has given way to service- and knowledge-based economic forces that require more specialized disciplinary and workforce training, especially in STEM-related areas. Policy, economic, business, and educational leaders have argued increasingly that a high-school diploma is no longer sufficient for successful individual entry into the contemporary U.S. economy and that at least some postsecondary education is needed, preferably equivalent to a baccalaureate degree.

To adapt to this (even now) transitioning economy, a considerable proportion of unemployed, underemployed, and unemployable laborers turned and are turning to their local community colleges. Lengthy absences from formal academic learning environments, however, position many of these returning students as lacking now-fundamental academic skills (e.g., study-based skills, technological fluency) or curricular background to succeed immediately within a higher education environment. This new climatic circumstance within U.S. higher education has fundamentally altered the relationship between K–12 public schooling, community colleges, four-year universities, and the U.S. economy.

Current students at both four-year colleges or universities and in some dual-enrollment high-school programs are opting for less expensive general-education courses at community colleges in order to reduce the growing costs of public and private university degree programs. As we explore more fully in the next sections, for all groups of students—both the so-called traditional and nontraditional student—remediation represents a significant and potentially challenging hurdle amid their transitions to college. And contrary to conventional reasoning, "many college students with limited academic skills do not take remedial coursework, while substantial numbers of students with strong high school backgrounds nevertheless take remedial courses."[12]

While most states reduced funding for higher education in the years following the 2007–10 recession, Republican governor Haslam of Tennessee led a bipartisan effort in the state legislature that made the state the first to offer free tuition for community or technical college to Tennessee high-school graduates. State leaders argued that the diminished levels of college graduates in the state would lead to future employment shortfalls as high-skilled jobs locate in the state. The central purpose of the Tennessee Promise Scholarship is to increase the number of college graduates within the state toward addressing potential shortages of skilled labor. Students are required to maintain a 2.0 grade point average, enroll full-time, and complete eight hours of community service during each semester in which they are enrolled. In conjunction with improving access to a postsecondary education, the scholarship also involves mentoring to support completion of the degree program.

The City of Chicago was next to follow in the free-tuition movement. Under Mayor Rahm Emanuel, Chicago became the first major city to adopt a program that defrayed the costs of attending community college. The City Colleges of Chicago, one of the largest community college systems in the nation, enrolls approximately 115,000 students annually. After initiating its Rejuvenation Plan in 2010, which involved reviewing and revising programs to support completion, graduation rates with the City Colleges climbed drastically.[13]

Anecdotally, however, these increases can be attributed partially to renewed efforts to encourage graduates who transferred to four-year institutions to officially claim the associates' degree that they earned but may not have declared upon transfer. City leaders believed that the community-college system could be an even larger tool for advancing higher education in an urban area and social advancement if more students could afford higher education. To increase access to a postsecondary education among graduates of Chicago Public Schools, the city developed the Chicago Star Scholarship. That program offers free tuition to attend community colleges for those students who maintained at least a 3.0 grade point average in high school and do not require remediation in math or English.[14]

Oregon, Minnesota, and Kentucky followed Tennessee in adopting state legislation offering financial waivers for residents to attend community college.[15] Similar legislation has been introduced in ten other state legislatures (Arizona, California, Washington, Oklahoma, Wisconsin, Illinois, Mississippi, New York, Massachusetts, and Maryland). Apart from Chicago, the only other major city to provide free community college tuition is Los Angeles.[16]

President Barack Obama had expressed a favorable view toward the free-tuition model. In 2015, he specifically acknowledged the important role of community colleges and proposed the American Graduation Initiative. The president set two national goals for higher education: (1) to outrank other countries by attaining the highest proportion of college graduates (2) and increase the number of community college graduates by 5 million before the year 2020.[17] This initiative in conjunction with funding provided by the Health Care and Reconciliation Act was intended to provide community colleges with the resources they needed to prepare Americans for the workforce.

President Obama also initiated a federal campaign to support free community college tuition for all graduates of U.S. high schools. In a speech at the Pellissippi State Community College in Knoxville, Tennessee, the president argued that free tuition would improve access to higher education and would support the development of a strong workforce without the burden of student loan debt.[18] Historically, public policy has focused on increasing access to higher education as a tool for economic development.

Following the economic recession of 2007–10, government at all levels continued to follow the suggestions of the Truman Commission by developing programs that make it easier for students to attend community colleges. While access is directly related to economic equality, graduation rates for community colleges across the nation remain low.[19] Tennessee experienced increases in student enrollments since offering free tuition; however, the effects on graduation rates remain insignificant.[20] Due to the infancy of the Chicago Star Scholarship, data regarding completion rates of students receiving free tuition are not yet available for analysis. In their pursuit of a postsecondary degree, many students are hindered by their obligation to successfully pass noncredit remediation, or development classes. Without addressing the structural factors preventing students from completing their associate's degree, the benefits of increased access and free tuition remain elusive.

CURRICULAR ISSUES IN THE COMMUNITY COLLEGE

As we have now argued, community colleges have long-standing and important status within the U.S. educational landscape, but in recent years at least, much of the ongoing commentary about community colleges involves controversies centering on cost, "college readiness," remediation, transfer, and completion rates. The community-college curriculum, however, is also a central consideration for any exploration into the evolution of the community college writ large and intersects with any of its other features. Exploring both the general curriculum and particularities of the community-college curriculum may shed light on commonplace assumptions about community colleges as ever-changing higher-educational institutions.

Documenting General Curricular Shifts

The community-college curriculum has been a consistent point of focus for educational researchers and reformers for most of the past century, with the first documented study being conducted as early as 1918.[21] The primary focus of these early studies was the distribution of course offerings as documented in two-year institutions' course catalogs.[22] Across those various studies, a central finding emerged and persisted through the 1970s: the prominence of the "academic" curriculum—that is, traditional liberal-arts subjects (e.g., natural sciences, humanities, modern languages)—began to and has continued to recede in favor of "non-academic offerings . . . [such as] commercial courses—which would presumably include trade and industrial training courses—[and these] made up the greatest percentage of the nonacademic curriculum, followed by engineering and home economics." This continual reconstitution of the community-college curriculum would expand even more through the midcentury, with more than 20 percent of community colleges offering nontraditional courses on health, music appreciation, social problems, world history, and art appreciation.[23] Liberal-arts subjects are certainly a mainstay within the curriculum, as well, but the need and capacity to expand the curriculum to adapt to broader societal shifts is a hallmark of the community-college curricular story.

Although the continued expansion of the community-college curriculum centered on the inclusion of so-called nonacademic subjects well through the 1990s, the discipline-centered focus of the curricular expansion began to shift toward courses that aligned with a renewed focused on science, technology, engineering, and mathematics (STEM). Given the broader push toward STEM preparation for an increasingly technologically oriented society and workforce, and especially in relation to the development and adoption of state- and national-level reforms to K–12 mathematics education, the heightening role of mathematics-specific courses especially should be scrutinized carefully.[24]

The Case of Developmental Mathematics Education

Community-college mathematics curriculum has changed more within the past ten years than it had within the preceding hundred years, but our central claim in this section is that community-college curricular reform remains for now in its infancy. There are remarkably few accounts in the research literature that document the curricular makeup and objectives of community-college mathematics education—or community-college curricula more broadly. Much of the existing scholarship has been "conducted by higher education scholars, and has focused on the costs of remediation or student retention and success, with success somewhat narrowly defined either as passing courses or as completing a college degree."[25] Much of our discussion here is intended to broaden that traditional focus and is derived from our professional experiences, intensive study of various programs across two- and four-year universities, and to the degree that it is possible, extant documentation of historical and contemporary curricular programs.

Traditional developmental education programs at community colleges typically follow a curricular sequence and content structure similar to the K–12 mathematics curriculum, taking the major learning objectives and content from elementary mathematics education (typically as a foundational mathematics course) through the course content of middle- and high-school algebra. Regardless of whether the format is in-person, online, or hybrid, the pedagogy of these courses typically follows a traditional "acquisitionist" perspective, where teaching and learning are conceptualized as a process of transmitting mathematical knowledge.[26] Instructor-centered, lecture-style teaching predominates, and the classroom environment centers on the demonstration of problems with the expectation that students complete versions of presented problems as homework outside of class.

Current Strategies and Projects for Curriculum Reform

In recent decades, research scholars and practitioner-scholars have worked together to develop and build a community dedicated to reforming the community-college curriculum, a community that has fostered some of the curricular reform projects discussed later in this section.[27] Although there is yet much to learn about the development, implementation, and outcomes of these reform efforts, the projects center on a discernable framework or set of principles and strategies. From our examination of these programs, each targets one or more of the following characteristics: sequence, structure, content, and pedagogy.

- Sequence-reform strategies target the outcomes of curricular trajectories and whether to offer more remediation, less, or none at all. With this approach, reformers center the relationship between the number of remedial courses taken and the increased probability that the student may fail or drop out.[28] These reforms often reduce the number of remedial courses to two, sometimes one. Some have also experimented with making mathematics remediation optional (e.g.,

Florida) or completely eliminating remediation programs in math, like Connecticut, which shifted mathematics remediation from a preparatory program to support courses that run concurrently to college-level courses.

- Structure-reform strategies focus on placement of content within the existing curricular structure; specifically whether institutions should either shift the remedial course content into existing credit-bearing courses or enroll students in credit-bearing courses while supporting the areas in need of remediation with supplementary support courses.
- Content-reform strategies center specifically on the subject-matter content of courses—for example, the glaring issue of algebra and that so few majors and careers utilize algebra or algebraic reasoning to any significant degree—and split mathematics remediation into different content-specific course pathways: one for those not transitioning to STEM fields without algebra, and the other for those transitioning to STEM fields with algebra.
- Pedagogical-reform strategies target the ways remedial courses are taught, integrating noncognitive research on engagement and motivation, such as the work on productive persistence and grit, along with curricular models that emphasize student-centered learning, questioning, and application.

Based on these varying reform strategies, numerous projects have emerged in community colleges across the United States. The following projects are prominent among those being implemented currently. For each, we present a broad overview of the reform, its category derived from the preceding list, and the effects of the reform (if available currently). It is important to note again that many of these reform programs are in early stages of implementation.

An Early Reform Project: New Life Model

Much of the reform for mathematics remedial programs in the community colleges originated in collaboration between foundations and education research centers, one of which was the American Mathematical Association of Two-Year Colleges (AMATYC). Their call for reform came through a sequence of documents describing the New Life Model.[29] This model includes sequence, structure, content, and pedagogical reform of remedial courses. It centers on two courses: mathematics literacy and algebraic literacy, depending on the students' trajectory—a major in a science, technology, engineering, or math field versus one that is non-STEM. This structure is now common across proposed reforms.

The two-course sequence appears new compared to the traditional beginning algebra to intermediate algebra sequence. The mathematics literacy course prepares students for the non-STEM trajectory, with no other remedial courses required. Students in the STEM trajectory take algebraic literacy or both mathematics literacy and algebraic literacy, depending on the level of remediation needed. In terms of content reform, the course builds off the assessment standards set in the National Research Council (NRC) text, *Adding It Up*, which is widely used in K–12 research.[30] This reform course also incorporates noncognitive standards that focus on the developing students' mathematics self-efficacy, motivation, and engagement. Pedagogical reform incorporates modeling, technology, and "instructional strategies that support student learning."

Curriculum Reform beyond Algebra

In response to the growing discourse in some circles that questions the importance of algebra as a course requirement for majors that do not employ algebraic reasoning, educational researchers and foundations have created remedial reform curricula that emphasize numeracy, quantitative reasoning, and real-world problem solving.[31] At the forefront stands Carnegie Foundation's Math Pathways projects, Quantway® and Statway®.[32]

Both serve as learning pathways that run alongside the traditional beginning algebra and intermediate algebra, serving as two-semester paths that accelerate students through their college-level math class. As opposed to AMATYC's model, which emphasizes mathematics literacy, Quantway and Statway emphasize quantitative literacy: Quantway emphasizes quantitative reasoning for those in liberal-arts majors, and Statway emphasizes statistical data analysis and reasoning for those with majors that require statistics. Both include noncognitive reforms focusing on engagement and motivation building out of productive persistence research.[33] Both include professional development for faculty to modify pedagogy and instruction, and both include language reform, focusing on teaching and texts that are more understandable for students. This suite of courses does not replace the algebraic, remedial sequence necessary for college algebra and STEM pathways.

The New Mathways Project

After collaboration with the Carnegie Foundation and AMATYC on reforms, the Dana Center launched the New Mathways Project (NMP) in collaboration with the Texas Association of Community Colleges.[34] As opposed to redesigning only structure or sequence, this project also focuses on curriculum. This curricular project moves away from the heavy algebraic focus of the traditional remedial sequences. It emphasizes classroom level change, institutional change, and cross-institutional reform.

The new four-credit course, similar in size and scope to individual remedial courses, focuses on mathematics literacy, quantitative reasoning, and problem solving. The only algebraic content students experience in their new course, Foundations of Mathematical Reasoning, is linear equations and modeling. The redesign shifts the algebraic content necessary for STEM pathways to college-level courses, restructuring the traditional college algebra course into a two-course sequence. This retains the algebraic reasoning and content necessary for student success in STEM while removing the barrier algebra represents for many remedial students.

Implemented now across most Texas community colleges, the reform is still in its infancy. However, initial published results are optimistic. Following a cohort of 233 students who began in Foundations of Mathematical Reasoning through their statistics course, 65 percent passed the remedial reform course, 46 percent continued the sequence into statistics, and 30 percent of the original cohort passed the statistics course.

Modularized Curriculum Projects

North Carolina and Virginia have radically redesigned the structure and sequence of mathematics remediation. In collaboration with the Community College Research Center (CCRC), the Analysis of Statewide Developmental Education Reform project adapted remedial math to become "a sequence of full-semester courses that covered a wide range of topics to shorter sequential modules, each of which covers a limited number of concepts."[35] In traditional remedial courses or other reforms, students can place into remedial courses even if they require remediation of one or two mathematical concepts. Modularizing the curriculum provides a more elegant solution to this issue, allowing students to remediate only the concepts necessary.

The project was designed with three goals: to decrease the number of students placing into remedial math courses; to reduce the time spent in the remedial sequence; and to align remedial curriculum to the college-level trajectories. Depending on the pathway, students are required to only take certain modules, with the most being required for the STEM pathway. In terms of curriculum, the system is based on mastery of the content, meaning students must achieve a certain percentage on assessments before moving on to the next concept. Also a pedagogical reform, this model requires computer-based classrooms, which require students to be more self-directed in and more responsible for their learning. Although this is also in its infancy, preliminary results are positive. In terms of placement rates, before the reform model was implemented at one community college in Virginia, 81 percent of students placed into remedial math in a fall 2010 cohort; after implementation, only 57 percent of students placed into remedial courses in fall 2012.[36]

CUNY Start. City University of New York's (CUNY) Start reform model is the only reform discussed here that is not community-college specific. It is mentioned here because it is gaining traction among administrations at community colleges as a potential reform model. This program grew out of a board decision in 1998 to eliminate remedial at CUNY.[37] Instead, students who place into remedial courses were directed to the city's several community colleges. CUNY Start grew out of this increased burden. It is an intensive, eight-week, twelve-credit program that is designed to prepare students to retake the placement for CUNY houses on several community colleges across the city. It specifically targets students who do not pass the pre-algebra and algebra sections of CUNY's placement test. As it is twelve credit hours, it represents a full-time course load for students, meaning it is designed to be the only course students take.

In terms of structure and curriculum, it replaces the beginning and intermediate algebra courses in the traditional, remedial sequence. It covers similar, algebraic content, and it incorporates noncognitive and student-centered components, such as preparing students for college by incorporating advising and student services into the course. It also includes pedagogical reform, as can be seen in CUNY Start's core values and teaching practices.[38] Pedagogical reform components include an emphasis on discovery learning, student-centered instruction, and questioning. In terms of access, it is unique in that the fee for the course is $35, and it includes free transportation for the full eight weeks of the course.

PERSPECTIVES ON ADMINISTRATIVE ISSUES: A VIGNETTE

Within the institutional structure of community colleges, administrators are often positioned between top-level policy making and the front lines of reforming curriculum, negotiating and implementing broad policies, managing instructional and human resources, and supporting students in various other ways. Furthermore, community-college administrators must juggle declining enrollments, changes in state funding, and in some cases, hiring or pay freezes. In contrast to the breadth of their work, there are remarkably few empirical studies or few first-person perspectives on how their responsibilities intersect with the many broader institutional concerns.[39] This section pivots from the tone and structure of the others in order to share the first-person perspective of one of the authors, John Bragelman, a former administrator of development education in one of the nation's largest urban community-college systems. Beginning with some personal background information, the following vignette emphasizes the interplay between institutional policy development and local administration, the centrality and importance of the community college's urban context, and the ways in which curricular and pedagogical reforms were implemented.[40]

After several years teaching high school and college classes, I served as director of developmental education at one of the seven City Colleges of Chicago (CCC). As the only person to ever serve in that position, I worked with the CCC's central district office, the administration, and the faculty to manage my college's remedial reform programs. The CCC district office governs the seven colleges collectively and administers centrally each college's separate, local administration. As a program director, I also reported to an associate dean and dean of academic affairs within my college. I worked primarily, however, to support my college's faculty. My primary responsibilities included developing and supporting a variety of programs, including supplemental tutoring, summer bridge programs (for high-school graduates), and community-building programs intended to assist returning adult students who were transitioning to college from the workforce or from other adult-life experiences. Although my academic content background is squarely in the fields of mathematics and mathematics education, as director of developmental education I worked with the English as a Second Language, (traditional) English, and mathematics departments.

In line with the differentiation generally among community colleges' missions, each college within the CCC system is associated with a specific career pathway or primary curricular focus. Similarly, the CCC system is varied also in terms of geographical focus, with colleges situated both within the central city and the downtown areas but also across the greater urban area as satellite neighborhood-based institutions. The primary curricular foci for the CCC campuses represent a broad curricular array: the various institutions specialize in areas such as human and natural sciences, advanced manufacturing, culinary arts and hospitality, health sciences, or—as was the case at the campus at which I worked as an administrator—college-to-career and business-industry emphases with an overarching focus on transfer to four-year universities. It is important to note that the sociopolitical realities of Chicago as a specific, urban context for the CCC and as one of the most segregated cities in the United States, especially with regard to race and socioeconomic class, play out across the CCC populations and varied campus cultures. Moreover, some of the CCC institutions serve predominantly Black or African American communities, others are predominantly Hispanic-serving institutions, while others within the same system—by virtue of their geographic positionality—are among the most diverse educational institutions within both the city and state.

Local policy making occurs at the college system or "district" level and is distributed to and implemented in the various colleges. In practice, these policies are intended to be enacted across the sites uniformly, despite the particular variations in campus culture and student body. When remedial reform is pushed at the college level, it results in a variety of implementations. Both have benefits and drawbacks. District-wide institutional reforms are translated locally as a "standardized" experience for students, even if many students attend multiple institutions within the city-college system simultaneously. Because standardized reform across institutional context is largely impossible, relative compliance becomes an institutional goal for local sites, and administrators are rewarded for the speed with which their offices respond to district-level policy pressures. Above all, speed of implementation is paramount.

At the time of my tenure as director, the CCC had one of the highest national rates of remediation and maintained consistently high attrition rates; pressure from the mayoral administration for reform was also immense and is likely to grow as new initiatives are proposed and take hold. A remarkably small percentage of students made it through the developmental mathematics sequence toward credit-bearing courses and graduation. As with institutions across the United States, the CCC administration focused on moving students through the development mathematics course sequence and into the gatekeeping sequence as quickly as possible. In regular administrative meetings, several questions were consistently raised: How fast can we get students to credit-level mathematics courses? How soon can said programmatic approach be implemented? How quickly can the new programmatic approach be launched? How quickly can the results be returned to the administration?

Along with internal institutional pressures faced by many community-college systems and their various local administrative structures, the broader higher-education policy terrain is also shifting in ways that may run counter to the concerns of two-year institutions and the communities they serve. This is, for instance, often the case for policies concerning remediation and transfer to four-year universities. As community colleges expand their enrollments and resources toward promoting transfer, four-year universities may (and sometimes do) enact policies that shift curricular requirements and tighten the transfer pipeline. Even as more institutions adopt requirements and courses that expand the disciplinary scope of entry-level courses—for instance, college-level quantitative reasoning courses in place of traditional, algebra-centered mathematics remediation courses—four-year colleges and universities are not required to accept these newer courses for transfer credit.

INSTRUCTORS

In recent years, there has been growing recognition that community-college faculty are themselves also at a crossroads—pulled in multiple directions by quickly shifting institutional directives and economic forces. Moreover, as Vilma Mesa and her colleagues argue, "the faculty at community colleges differ in key ways from K–12 teachers and from other higher education faculty," including greater likelihood of being from underrepresented groups, balancing their community-college teaching responsibilities with other professional obligations outside of their institution, or teaching courses across multiple campuses or institutions.[41] Yet, a growing commonality among community-college faculty is that they are increasingly part-time, contingent members of their institutions' workforces, with almost no job security and relatively little institutional support. Especially in the case of developmental education (mathematics again being primary among these subjects), this often means that the instructional faculty are more likely to have the least experience teaching their subject matter and fewer institutionalized opportunities for professional development and mentoring.

Reported recently by the Center for Community College Student Engagement (CCCSE), part-time instructors teach 58 percent of all U.S. community-college classes and are generally regarded and operate as a separate grouping apart from their full-time colleagues.[42] As "contingent" faculty, their collective marginalization has become "a fundamental feature of the economic model that sustains community college education" and consequently the "least expensive way to deliver instruction."[43] Moreover, this expanding group of faculty are routinely assigned to teach the lowest-level, highest-need courses within the community-college curriculum; for instance, development education faculty are much more likely to be part-time instructors with fewer than ten years of teaching experience.[44]

Although there has been growing (and much needed) attention to the looming crisis associated with the disproportionate emergence of part-time instructional faculty at both community colleges and four-year institutions, the extent of the deprofessionalization and lack of developmental support has and will continue to have a detrimental impact on the quality of classroom interactions. One very practical element of this—particularly regarding developmental mathematics courses—is the need to support community-college instructors toward adopting contemporary pedagogical approaches. Specifically, community-college instruction in mathematics should shift from instructors being classically trained "content experts" who deliver content to students (who are expected to consume it) to "domain guides" who are tasked with guiding students' participation in mathematical exploration, problem solving, and ultimately, toward problem-posing pedagogy.[45] This kind of shift, however, requires considerable institutional investment in the professional development of faculty and a continued commitment to exploring and exposing faculty to new pedagogical approaches.

STUDENTS AS LEARNERS RATHER THAN AS CONSUMERS

Traditionally, community colleges have served students by offering opportunities to learn transferable content knowledge or to learn career-oriented skills—and have been a "primary point of postsecondary entry for underrepresented and disadvantaged students."[46] As related throughout this chapter, there has been a considerable shift in how community-college policy, curriculum, instruction, and those responsible for each are viewed systemically. Curriculum has shifted from representing the content trajectory that teachers draw from in their instruction and that students are expected to know and be able to do toward platforms that deliver content to passive recipients. In the traditional sense, instructors are increasingly contingent faculty laborers and managers of these evolving curricular platforms. In much the same way, the role of student has shifted contemporarily from the student as a returning learner to the student as a consumer of institutional course offerings and support services.

In the student-as-consumer paradigm, "student success" has become the primary institutional goal and is largely "to be understood as composed of two possibly interrelated aspects: students learning the material that teachers and departments intend them to learn and students making steady progress toward accomplishing their academic goals."[47] Progression through the institutional curriculum, however, is not the same as learning, yet the former is often emphasized above the latter.

One of the looming issues with the students-as-consumer paradigm is that it largely obscures the psychosocial elements of learning—issues of motivation, persistence, identity, and the contingencies of social group membership. But from emerging studies of adult learning in remedial mathematics contexts, there is evidence that students are negotiating themselves as racialized and gendered learners inasmuch as they are negotiating the course content.[48] Furthermore, there is growing research that suggests that learners in these context are reconstructing their identities as classroom learners—especially for students who return to the classroom after years in the workforce—and that this process may involve navigating identity threats and other so-called noncognitive aspects of learning (although they are surely linked to cognition).

Specifically regarding development education courses, recent studies suggest that development mathematics courses particularly may bring about unintended and threatening effects on student learning and, more broadly, students' mathematical proficiency. Although many of these and other related policy documents decry the growth of remediation in mathematics amid the transition to postsecondary coursework, the recommendations of these documents have had modest discernable influence on the broader debate.[49] The tension regarding developmental mathematics courses is typically centered on completion rates, costs, and institutional missions, whereas the question of whether these courses influence students' learning of mathematics—and students' much-needed proficiency in the subject—is largely absent.

As the NRC *Adding It Up* report asserts, however, it is crucially important for *all* students to learn mathematics successfully—and that doing so involves much more than the accumulation or rehashing of mathematical skills and concepts. The report's framework specifies five interwoven strands that contribute to proficiency in mathematics: conceptual understanding, procedural fluency, adaptive reasoning, strategic competence, and productive disposition. Along with conceptual understanding and procedural fluency, adaptive reasoning and strategic competence describe aspects of mathematical processes in which students should engage. Productive disposition, however, describes the affective aspect of mathematics learning, emphasizing that learners should develop a "habitual inclination to see mathematics as sensible, useful, and worthwhile, coupled with the belief in diligence and one's own efficacy."[50]

Typically, developmental mathematics courses tend to place unusually burdensome emphasis on procedural fluency, or the capacity to carry out computational methods flexibly, accurately, and efficiently. The underlying assumption is that students who exhibit underperformance on placement exams and are subsequently placed in NCBR (non–credit-bearing remedial) mathematics courses necessarily lack the requisite procedure-driven skills that are foundational to algebra. To a lesser extent, these courses may incorporate the other conceptual or process-oriented aspects of proficiency, but there has been no attentiveness in research or practice to the influence of NCBR mathematics courses on students' dispositions or their identities as mathematics learners. Specifically, we know little about the potential psychosocial threats or damage that NCBR mathematics courses may pose for students who either succeed or struggle. In short, many ask if the courses are effective or "successful"—if they *work*. But we have generally not asked whether the very *experiences* of these kinds of courses are damaging for students in other ways.

CONCLUSIONS AND IMPLICATIONS

This chapter offers a multilevel perspective on the contemporary community college—from its originating mission, to federal and local attempts to bolster that mission, to the central actors who implement these policy and curricular aims toward serving students and their communities. Along with this primary focus, we explore the specific contexts of urban community colleges and the content-specific domain of developmental mathematics education. In an undercurrent, we argue throughout this chapter that the contemporary community college follows a tradition of shaping its curricular and pedagogical aims with regard to two primary missions: differentiation and access. With regard to differentiation, community colleges serve the broader higher-education enterprise by preserving the high-status missions of four-year colleges and universities. With regard to access, community colleges have also explicitly served local communities by providing a stepping-stone to the social-mobility mechanism that higher education more broadly supports.

Contemporarily, community colleges have reemerged within federal policy, most notably through Obama administration initiatives and state-based efforts to promote access and tuition support for prospective community-college students. As with recent waves of curricular reform, these recent policy efforts are too new to assess effectively. However, the spirit of these policies suggest that federal and local attention to the need to expand access to community colleges for today's returning student population and traditional undergraduate population is growing at great speed.

In lieu of explicit recommendations, there are implications across these levels that would support the open-door access mission of the community college and the broader need for community colleges to promote economic development in urban communities. First, we recognize that, in the contemporary community college, transfer to four-year colleges and universities remains a major institutional objective but may not be as primary as it once was. This is not to suggest that students should not strive to transfer to baccalaureate-granting institutions, but that community colleges are recalibrating their offerings with less attention to students' intentions to transfer. Furthermore, we recognize that curricular and policy reforms are still in early stages of implementation, and the promise of community-college access will only grow.

Notes

Direct correspondence to Gregory V. Larnell, Department of Curriculum and Instruction, University of Illinois at Chicago, 1040 West Harrison Street (MC 147), Chicago, IL 60607, glarnell@uic.edu.

This chapter was authored jointly, whereas the first author was the primary contributor and contributions are shared equally among the second and third authors. The first author acknowledges support from the UIC College of Urban Planning and Public Affairs and, on other current projects, the National Science Foundation, the UIC Institute for Research on Race and Public Policy, and the UIC College of Education. The second author acknowledges support on other projects by the Loyola University Chicago Gannon Center for Women and Leadership. Portions of this chapter appear, are based on, or have been presented in the UIC Research on Urban Education Policy Initiative Policy Brief Series, the *Journal of Urban Mathematics Education*, and the Mathematical Sciences Research Institute (Berkeley, California) Critical Issues Series. Any opinions or errors herein are attributable only to the authors and not any of the aforementioned institutions.

The epigraph is from Jerome Karabel, "Community Colleges and Social Stratification," *Harvard Educational Review* 42, no. 4 (1972): 530.

1. Peter Riley Bahr, Christie Toth, Kathryn Thirolf, and Johanna C. Massé, "A Review and Critique of the Literature on Community College Students' Transition Process and Outcomes in Four-Year Institutions," in *Higher Education: Handbook of Theory and Research*, ed. M. B. Paulsen, 459–511 (Dordrecht, Germany: Springer, 2013); U.S. Census Bureau, "The 2012 Statistical Abstract," accessed July 25, 2016, www2.census.gov/library/publications/2011/compendia/statab/131ed/tables/educ.pdf.

2. Stephen G. Katsinas and Terrance A. Tollefson, as cited in Sara Goldrick-Rab, "Challenges and Opportunities for Improving Community College Student Success," *Review of Educational Research* 80, no. 2 (2010): 438.

3. "Community College Completion: Progress toward 50% Increase," American Association of Community Colleges, 2015, accessed August 2, 2015, www.aacc.nche .edu/AboutCC/Trends/Documents/completion_report_05212015.pdf.

4. Gregory V. Larnell, "More than Just Skill: Examining Mathematics Identities, Racialized Narratives, and Remediation among Black Undergraduates," *Journal of Research in Mathematics Education* 47, no. 3 (2016): 233–69; Gregory V. Larnell, "We Real Cool: Reconsidering the Cooling-Out Phenomenon in a Mathematics Education Context," unpublished manuscript, 2016.

5. Clifford Adelman, *Principal Indicators of Student Academic Histories in Postsecondary Education, 1972–2000*, U.S. Department of Education and the Institute of Education Sciences, January 2004, www2.ed.gov/rschstat/research/pubs/prinindicat/ prinindicat.pdf.

6. Josh M. Beach, *Gateway to Opportunity: A History of Community College in the United States* (Sterling, VA: Stylus, 2011); Arthur M. Cohen, Florence B. Brawer, and Carrie B. Kisker, *The American Community College* 6th ed (San Francisco: Jossey-Bass, 1982).

7. Beach, *Gateway to Opportunity*, 9.

8. Ibid.

9. Cohen et al., *American Community College*.

10. Philo Hutcheson, "The Truman Commission's Views of the Future," *Thought and Action* 23 (2007): 107–15.

11. Claire Krendl Gilbert and Donald E. Heller, "Access, Equity, and Community Colleges: The Truman Commission and Federal Higher Education Policy from 1947 to 2011," *Journal of Higher Education* 84, no. 3 (2013): 417–43.

12. Paul A. Attewell, David E. Lavin, Thurston Domina, and Tania Levey, "New Evidence on College Remediation," *Journal of Higher Education* 77, no. 5 (2006): 914.

13. "City Colleges of Chicago Fact Sheet," City Colleges of Chicago, 2016, accessed July 18, 2016, www.ccc.edu/menu/Pages/City-Colleges-of-Chicago-Fact-Sheet-.aspx.

14. "Chicago Star Scholarship," City Colleges of Chicago, 2015, accessed July 18, 2016, www.ccc.edu/departments/Pages/chicago-star-scholarship.aspx.

15. "Free Community College," National Conference of State Legislatures, April 25, 2016, accessed July 25, 2016, www.ncsl.org/research/education/free-community -college.aspx.

16. Eric Garcetti, "2016 State of the City 2016," mayor's office, Los Angeles, accessed July 27, 2016, www.lamayor.org.

17. The White House, "Building American Skills through Community Colleges," 2016, accessed April 23, 2017, https://obamawhitehouse.archives.gov/issues/education/ higher-education/building-american-skills-through-community-colleges.

18. President Barack Obama, "President Obama Remarks on Higher Education," speech presented at the Pellissippi State Community College, January 9, 2015, accessed July 27, 2016, www.c-span.org/video/?323697-1/president-obama-vice-president -biden-remarks-tennessee#.

19. Beach, *Gateway to Opportunity*.

20. Alana Semuels, "Free Tuition Is Not Enough," *Atlantic*, October 15, 2015, accessed July 24, 2016, www.theatlantic.com.

21. Gwyer Schuyler, "A Historical and Contemporary View of the Community College Curriculum," *New Directions for Community Colleges* 1999, no. 108 (1999): 3–15.

22. Walter Crosby Eels, *The Junior College* (Boston: Houghton Mifflin, 1931).

23. Schuyler, "Historical and Contemporary View," 4.

24. Gregory Larnell, "More than Just Skill: Examining Mathematics Identities, Racialized Narratives, and Remediation among Black Undergraduates," *Journal of Research in Mathematics Education* 47, no. 3 (2016): 233–69.

25. Vilma Mesa, Claire Wladis, and Laura Watkins, "Research Problems in Community College Mathematics Education: Testing the Boundaries of K–12 Research," *Journal for Research in Mathematics Education* 45, no. 2 (2014): 173–92, 174.

26. Anna Sfard, "On Two Metaphors for Learning and the Dangers of Choosing Just One," *Educational Researcher* 27, no. 2 (1998): 4–13, 4.

27. See, for example, Katherine Stephenson, "Developmental Mathematics: For Whom? To What End?," *Critical Issues in Mathematics Education* 11, no. 12 (Berkeley, CA: Mathematical Sciences Research Institute, March 2015).

28. Paul Fain, "Remediation If You Want It," *Inside Higher Ed* (2013); Paul Fain, "Low Expectations, High Stakes," *Inside Higher Ed* (2014).

29. Jack Rotman, "Inside New Life: A Grand Vision for Developmental Mathematics," *MathAMATYC Educator* 4, no. 3 (2013): 27–35.

30. National Research Council Mathematics Learning Study Committee, *Adding It Up: Helping Children Learn Mathematics* (Washington, DC: National Academies Press, 2001).

31. On the question of the importance of algebra, see Andrew Hacker, *The Math Myth: And Other STEM Delusions* (New York: New Press, 2016).

32. Katherine K. Mcrseth, "Update: Report on Innovations in Developmental Mathematics—Moving Mathematical Graveyards," *Journal of Developmental Education* 34, no. 3 (2011): 32–33, 36–38, 32; Hiroyuki Yamada, "Community College Pathways' Program Success: Assessing the First Two Years' Effectiveness of Statway," Carnegie Foundation for the Advancement of Teaching, 2014.

33. Carol Dweck, Gregory M. Walton, and Geoffrey L. Cohen, *Academic Tenacity: Mindsets and Skills that Promote Long-Term Learning* (Seattle, WA: Bill and Melinda Gates Foundation, 2011).

34. Elizabeth Zachry Rutschow and John Diamond, "Laying the Foundations: Early Findings from the New Mathways Project," MDRC, April 2015.

35. Hoori Santikian Kalamkarian, Julia Raufman, and Nikki Edgecombe, "Statewide Developmental Education Reform: Early Implementation in Virginia and North Carolina," Community College Research Center, Teachers College, Columbia University, May 2015, 1.

36. Olga Rodríguez, "Increasing Access to College-Level Math: Early Outcomes Using the Virginia Placement Test," Community College Research Center, Teachers College, Columbia University, 2014.

37. William Trombley, "Remedial Education under Attack," *National Crosstalk* 6, no. 3 (1998): 1.

38. "CUNY Start Math—Core Values and Teaching Practices," CUNY Start, City University of New York, December 9, 2013, www2.cuny.edu/wp-content/uploads/sites/4/media-assets/CSCoreValuesandPracticesMath12092013.pdf; Thomas Bailey and Shanna Smith Jaggars, "When College Students Start Behind: College Completion Series: Part Five," Report Higher Education, Century Foundation, June 2, 2016, https://tcf.org/content/report/college-students-start-behind/; Drew Allen and Aaron Horenstein, *CUNY Start: Analysis of Student Outcomes*, Office of Academic Affairs, City University of New York, November 2013, www.cuny.edu/academics/evaluation/reports/CUNYStartStudyFall13.pdf.

39. For exceptions, see Stephenson, "Developmental Mathematics"; John Bragelman, "Praxis as Dialogue: Teacher and Administrator," *Journal of Urban Mathematics Education* 8, no. 2 (2015): 27–43.

40. Personal information related in Bragelman, "Praxis as Dialogue."

41. Mesa et al., "Research Problems," 176. Center for Community College Student Engagement, *Contingent Commitments: Bringing Part-Time Faculty into Focus* (Austin: University of Texas at Austin, Program in Higher Education Leadership, 2014).

42. John E. Roueche, *Strangers in Their Own Land: Part-Time Faculty in American Community Colleges* (Annapolis, MD: AACC Publications, 1995).

43. Center for Community College Student Engagement, *Contingent Commitments*, 2.

44. Ibid.; Mesa et al., "Research Problems."

45. Gregory V. Larnell, Erika C. Bullock, and Christopher C. Jett, "Rethinking Teaching and Learning Mathematics for Social Justice from a Critical Race Perspective," *Journal of Education* 196, no. 1 (2016): 19 29.

46. Bahr et al., "Review and Critique," 460.

47. Mesa et al., "Research Problems," 181.

48. See, for example, Larnell, "More than Just Skill"; Gregory V. Larnell, Denise Boston, and John Bragelman, "The Stuff of Stereotypes: Toward Unpacking Identity Threats amid African American Students' Learning Experiences," *Journal of Education* 194, no. 1 (2014): 49–57.

49. For one such policy document, see National Research Council Mathematics Learning Study Committee, *Adding It Up*.

50. National Research Council Mathematics Learning Study Committee, *Adding It Up*, 5.

The Millennials

BRAD HARRINGTON

Much has been written and said about the so-called Millennial generation. Perhaps no generation has spawned more articles, books, and blogs than our present crop of young adults aged eighteen to thirty-six. Further, perhaps no generation has been saddled with more labels, clichés, and stereotypes than the very large cohort of professionals who have entered the workforce since the turn of the twenty-first century. Generational "experts" have variously asserted that this group is driven, lazy, hard-working, entitled, ambitious, self-centered, socially responsible, disloyal, and committed—take your pick. It seems that if you apply enough contradictory labels to any large group of individuals, some of those are bound to be accurate at least some of the time, or at least they will have the ring of truth to those who are disposed to that point of view. But this hardly equates to knowledge grounded in rigorous research.

The insurgence of millennial thinking followed the 2000 publication of William Strauss and Neil Howe's *Millennials Rising: The Next Great Generation*.[1] This book and others like it spawned a cottage industry of generational scholars. These experts and consultants asserted that the Millennials were truly different than the generations that preceded them and they could be described by a common set of traits that were based on the times and manner in which they were raised.

But generalizations about large groups of people, especially those connected only by arbitrary birth-date categories, are bound to be fraught with problems. In his excellent "The Millennial Muddle" in 2009, journalist Eric Hoover points out that to accept generational thinking one must "swallow two large assumptions":

- that tens of millions of people born over a twenty-year period are fundamentally different from people of other age groups
- that those tens of millions are similar to one another in meaningful ways

There is reason to believe that the times in which we are raised and the accompanying societal and economic trends do impact us, our thinking, and our values on such central issues as our work, our well-being, and our families. Researchers have explored trends that have impacted the present generation of young adults but these need to be better understood. They include, for example, the increasing pervasiveness and impact of technology, changing gender roles, a changing employment contract, the changing nature of work and careers, and delays in making "adult commitments."[2]

These macro-trends have doubtless impacted this generation just as other societal and historical trends have impacted previous generations. But the question is, to what extent? And can these trends or other factors explain the dramatic differences and provocative labels that have been attached to this cohort?

SOCIETAL TRENDS THAT HAVE IMPACTED MILLENNIALS

A number of macro-trends have made life for young adults in the early twenty-first century different, and perhaps more challenging in many ways, than was the case for previous generations. Four major trends have changed life and the workplace for this young generation: the increasing impact of technology, delaying adult commitments, changing gender roles, and the changing nature and expectations of careers and the workplace.

Technology's Growing Impact

One trend that has profoundly changed life for Millennials in the United States is the pervasive availability and use of technology. Young adults have grown up in a world that allows, and even seems to demand, nearly constant interaction with technological devices. The desktop computers and cell phones of the early 2000s have been replaced by smartphones and other portable, internet-capable devices that give users access to information at their fingertips at all times.[3] Smartphones, in particular, have become the technology of choice for most Millennials. In 2004, 65 percent of U.S. adults owned a cell phone; 92 percent owned one in 2015; and smartphone ownership increased from 35 percent in 2011 to 68 percent in 2015.[4]

According to the U.S. Chamber of Commerce, Millennials are 2.5 times more likely "to be early adopters of technology" than members of previous generations, and they display high levels of technological fluency as a result of their regular use and exposure. This high level of utilization has drastically impacted the way in which Millennials gather information, communicate with others, work, and experience and interact with the world around them.[5]

While the pervasive presence and use of technology in our day-to-day lives is undisputable, researchers are still determining to what extent technology impacts our social lives and relationships with others. While there is consensus that technology has expanded the range and speed of our communications, there remains significant debate among scholars regarding the positive and negative effects of technology. Researchers, such as MIT's Sherry Turkle, argue that the "new mediated life has gotten us into trouble." Turkle asserts that acts such as text messaging serve not as a means of forming a social bond but rather are actually "flight[s] from conversation." Often scripted, edited, and planned, these technological conversations lack the "open-ended and spontaneous" elements of conversation that allow us to show our more "vulnerable" and "fully present" selves. Turkle posits that the widespread integration—or perhaps, intrusion—of technology into nearly all of our professional and personal interactions has resulted in "an assault on empathy," whereby the "conversations where empathy and intimacy flourish and social action gains strength" are effectively eradicated.[6]

By contrast, scholars Jennifer J. Deal, David G. Altman, and Steven G. Roselberg point to some of the positive aspects of technology and the social exchanges that its usage enables. Social media platforms have "made it easier for people to interact with each other synchronously and asynchronously, regardless of where they live in the world, and to participate in communities of similar interest and practice." The increased connectivity that results from such platforms is presumably a boon in both business and personal contexts. Yet the authors also cite evidence arguing "the human brain cannot effectively integrate multiple inputs at the same time."[7] This would perhaps suggest that one sacrifices quality for quantity: as the potential for human connection and interaction exponentially increases, so too does the possibility of being overwhelmed and overstimulated. This assertion may be supported by statistics that show that 67 percent of smartphone owners "find themselves checking their phone for messages, alerts or calls—even when they don't notice their phone ringing or vibrating." A surprising 44 percent have slept with their phone next to their bed, and 29 percent can't imagine life without their phone.[8]

Delaying Commitments

Another distinguishing feature of Millennials is their proclivity for delaying commitments that have traditionally marked the major milestones of adulthood. From attaining a "career job," to marriage and child rearing to the purchase of homes, many Millennials have postponed these rites of passage into adulthood. While critics suggest that these delays are indications of Millennials' failures to commit or "failure to launch"—to cite the title of a popular 2006 film on this issue—the reasons for so doing are wide-ranging and complex.

One reason cited for Millennials delaying major life decisions and commitments is the significant student loan debt that many Millennials accrued as a result of attending postsecondary institutions. The same 2012 U.S. Chamber of Commerce study cited above asserts that Millennials "are sizing up to be the most educated generation in history" but this high level of education has come at a significant cost.[9] The *Boston Globe* reported in 2015 that student loan debt had "tripled over the past decade," climbing to an astonishing $1.232 trillion. Citing the Federal Reserve Bank of New York, the report claims that student debt "now accounts for a larger share of household debt than credit card, auto loan, and all other forms of debt, except for mortgages."[10] While research estimates that Millennials with a college degree earn, on average, about $17,500 more than their peers with high-school diplomas, the amount of debt that a Millennial assumes in completing a bachelor's degree averages around $35,000.[11]

Yet, the high cost of higher education and the accompanying debt have not been a significant deterrent to young adults seeking it, possibly because of an ever-increasing number of jobs that require a bachelor's degree and the stated improved salaries for college graduates. Research indicates that only those employees who have a bachelor's degree "experienced an increase in earnings over the last generation," highlighting one of the crucial impetuses that continues to motivate college attendance despite its rising cost.[12]

There is also clear evidence that Millennials significantly delay commitments to marriage and having children compared to previous generations. Part of this "delay" can in fact be explained by the increased number of years the average U.S. student spends in higher education. Recent research suggests that only 19 percent of full-time students attain their bachelor's degree in four years with a "benchmark" of six years increasingly coming to define the norm.[13]

Today in the United States, the average age for a "first marriage is 27 for women and 29 for men," compared to 1960 when the average age was 20 for women and 23 for men.[14] While many Millennials opt to simply delay marriage, a significant number choose to cohabitate (and/or rear children) without marrying. Indeed, nearly a quarter (or 24%) of "never-married young adults" from the age of twenty-five to thirty-four cohabitate with a partner. This compares with 1960 figures, where only 9 percent of adults of the same age who had never married cohabitated. Although it can be difficult to pinpoint the deeply personal reasons motivating marriage (or lack thereof), some researchers have posited financial security as a deciding factor in Millennials' delayed marriage commitments, as well as a more pervasive view of marriage as less socially important.[15]

Changing Gender Roles

Today, women earn the majority of bachelor's, master's, and doctoral degrees in the United States, including approximately 60 percent of degrees awarded at the undergraduate level.[16] In 2012, 44 percent of young women between the ages of eighteen and twenty-four were enrolled in bachelor's degree or graduate programs, compared to 38 percent of men in the same age group.[17]

Women's larger representation in higher education has translated into women's increased presence and participation in the workplace. Women now make up nearly half (47%) of the entire labor force, compared to 1970, when women accounted for 38 percent. Young women's earnings today "are more than 90 percent of men's" earnings, which is higher than women workers between the ages of thirty-five and sixty-four, whose earnings are 80 percent "or less" than what men earn "across the board."[18] Women are also well-represented in nearly all professional and managerial jobs, with the exception of engineering professions. This is not the case, however, for roles in the most senior management ranks, especially in private industry where they account for only 15 percent of director level roles and 4 percent of CEO roles in the Fortune 1000.[19]

In one-quarter of dual-career couples' households, wives earn more than their husbands. In fact, women are now the primary breadwinners in two out of five U.S. households.[20] These striking figures call into question some of our long-held stereotypes about men as breadwinners and women as primarily responsible for children and the home. In fact, 78 percent of married Millennial men have a working spouse, versus 47 percent of baby boomers.[21] A majority of Millennial men believe that they will have partners who also have careers and who view the roles as both a parent and a professional as roles that will be shared.[22]

There is also growing evidence that young women are now more professionally ambitious than their male counterparts. Research indicates that 66 percent of women aged eighteen to thirty-four rate having a career "high on their list of priorities," whereas only 59 percent of their male counterparts stated the same. Such figures are an increase from a 1997 Pew Research Center study, which asserted that 56 percent of young women and 58 percent of young men placed high importance on attaining a career.[23]

These trends have led researchers to underscore the importance of accommodating these shifting gender and professional values through innovative workplace practices. As researchers Morley Winograd and Michael D. Hais argue, "with both parents equally involved in career and family, employers who wish to attract top talent will have no other choice but to accommodate the [Millennial] generation's demand for such things as telecommuting, flexible hours, and child care."[24]

Changing Expectations about Careers and the Workplace

Social, economic, and organizational forces over the past three decades have resulted in an altered career landscape. These changes have duly influenced Millennials' expectations for their employers and the professional paths they envision for themselves.

In the last two decades of the twentieth century, job security for professional employees, once viewed as standard for leading employers, came under threat as an organizational value. While for most of the century U.S. labor practices had been targeted to creating more lasting relationships between employers and employees, by 1980 the labor market started to become increasingly characterized by layoffs and downsizing. Much of this shift resulted from dramatic improvements in technology and automation that eliminated many manufacturing and clerical functions as well as the rise of outsourcing jobs to developing countries. In his book *The Disposable American*, *New York Times* journalist Louis Uchitelle argues that, as layoffs became more standard, the failure that they signified began to be increasingly internalized by the laid-off workers themselves rather than identified as a failure of management, as had been the view in earlier days. This shift resulted in what Uchitelle identifies as a pervasive individual anxiety that has serious consequences for the worker and companies alike: "layoffs damage companies by undermining the productivity of those who survive but feel vulnerable, as well as the productivity of those who are laid off and get jobs again. All lose some of the commitment, trust, and collegial behavior that stable employment or the expectation of stable employment normally engenders."[25]

At the same time, notable increases in the cost of living—driven mainly by dramatic rises in housing, health care, and higher-education costs—also meant that fewer families could rely on one income to service the family's needs.[26] As a result, it was no longer possible for one spouse to focus solely on his or her professional life because most spouses do not have someone at home who can focus solely on personal and family matters. Therefore, the issue of work-life balance came into greater focus as employees increasingly tried to create work structures and schedules that were synergistic with their personal and family lives.[27]

With these developments came a shift in career patterns with less hierarchical, rigid, and stable career paths and a greater need for employees to manage their own careers rather than assuming that the organization would do that for them. Organizational instability and downsizing has led individuals to regard their career more as a series of jobs rather than as a standardized progression on one particular path or through one particular organization. It has also led organizations to create more customized approaches to career planning and career structures. In these scenarios, the individual assumes an increasing amount of responsibility in ensuring that both personal and career goals are attained, and certain features of the job, such as flexibility, assume a position of much greater importance.[28]

Perhaps such structural changes in the U.S. workforce explain, in part, why Millennials have been stereotyped as a job-hopping generation. There is much debate about the validity of this perspective. Indeed, FiveThirtyEight's Ben Casselman recently argued that Millennials, whose entrance into a post-recession job market might have done irrevocable damage to their lifelong earning potential, don't switch jobs nearly enough.[29] This position is echoed by Jeanne Meister, who claims that faster promotions, acquiring new skills, and self-protection against layoffs are among the benefits for Millennials who job-hop.[30] Whether they frequently change jobs or not, however, it is important to distinguish job-hopping from career changes, where Millennials would need to acquire an entirely new skill set or partake in professional training programs in order to embark on a new professional path altogether. Currently, there does not appear to be conclusive evidence that would suggest that Millennials frequently change careers or industry affiliation or do so at a higher rate than previous generations.

As mentioned earlier, the rise and pervasive availability of low cost, distributed technologies and the internet, along with the rapid expansion of increasingly global organizations, has changed when and where people work. This, in concert with dual-career families, has led many employers and their employees to agree that flexible approaches to working are not merely acceptable but desirable for all parties. In June 2016, *CNN.com* featured the headline "Dell (Computer) really wants you to work from home . . . if you want to." The article stated that 25 percent of Dell's employees work from home full- or part-time, and the company's goal is to achieve 50 percent by 2020. The reasons? To lower real estate costs, save employees valuable time, and reduce the company's carbon footprint by lowering traffic congestion.[31] Flexible workplaces and flexible careers are fast becoming the norm in many workplaces (e.g., IBM, Aetna, Humana, American Express, and United Health Group), and this more agile and adaptable organization seems to be in synch with the desire of many Millennials for greater control over what they do and how they do it.

Finally, trends in geographic mobility distinguish Millennials' work experience from other generations. A 2014 Bloomberg report notes that Millennials are less likely to move away from their hometowns than previous generations. While the reasons for so doing are varied, the report suggests that "a combination of relatively low-paying opportunities, the burden of student loans and an aversion to taking risks" are the primary factors in many Millennials' decision to stick close to home. While adults under the age of thirty-five have traditionally been the most likely of any age group in the United States to move, analysis of U.S. Census Data, undertaken by William Frey of the Brookings Institution, reveals that, starting around 2013, only 20.2 percent of young adults aged twenty-four to thirty-four relocated, which is "the lowest rate for that age group in data going back to 1947, down from 35 percent in 1965."[32]

It is important to acknowledge, however, that despite Millennials' ostensible aversion to relocating, some of the factors noted above are expressions of social anxieties regarding the state of the job market and thus do not necessarily reflect the preferences that Millennials may have as far as where they would like to live and work. Indeed, a 2014 *New York Times* article looks at the "exodus" of young adults moving from suburban areas into urban centers like New York City and staying there. While the cost of living in cities like New York is oftentimes much higher than in surrounding suburbs, researchers argue that easier commutes to work and access to cultural institutions, bars, and restaurants are some of the reasons that Millennials are choosing to remain in urban areas.[33] Additionally, a 2015 report from the American Institute of Economic Research found that Millennials with bachelor's degrees are attracted to urban areas with, first and foremost, "high density of people with a college degree, a low unemployment rate, and the ability to get around the city without a car." Ranking slightly lower on the scale of importance were salary, rent expenses, and competition for educated young adults jobs.

This has made cities such as Washington, D.C., San Francisco, and Boston (in addition to New York City) some of the most popular geographic locations for Millennials who choose to relocate.[34]

WHAT MILLENNIALS WANT FROM WORK: A RESEARCH STUDY

The Boston College Center for Work & Family embarked on a research study to better understand how Millennials make career choices, define success, and manage the balance between their professional and personal life goals. We also sought to understand what organizational qualities or characteristics Millennials find the most appealing and what organizational strategies best facilitate employee development and engagement.

The study targeted individuals aged twenty-two to thirty-five who had at least two years of professional work experience and who were employed at one of five large companies. All five employers were members of the Boston College Workforce Roundtable and, as such, might be seen as having "progressive workforce management approaches." The study used a mixed-methods approach. Initially, interviews were conducted with twenty-six individuals to gain a better understanding of Millennials' career and work-life goals and attitudes. An analysis of the qualitative data was then used as a basis for developing the questions used in the quantitative survey that targeted a much larger sample of Millennial employees.

The survey was conducted online in each of the five companies. All of the companies were multinational, but we limited the research to employees working in the United States. The organizations we engaged were in the insurance, banking, accounting, and consulting sectors. A total of 1,100 employees completed the survey across the five companies, ranging from 95 to 323 responses from each of the participating organizations. The companies' employee databases were used to randomly select participants who met the study criteria, and all employees' participation in the study was voluntary.

The study was focused on a "white-collar," college-educated population working in large enterprises. As such, the results of the study are not nationally representative. The large sample size does, however, lend credibility to the results, albeit with a limited population. Some relevant demographics of the sample include the following:

- 56 percent of survey participants were women and 44 percent were men
- 62 percent were in the 30–35 age group, and 38 percent were aged 22–29; the median age was 31

- the median number of years of work experience was eight
- 99 percent worked full-time
- 29 percent of participants were managers, 64 percent salaried professionals, and 7 percent were paid hourly
- 67 percent of study participants had achieved a bachelor's degree as their highest educational level, 25 percent a master's degree, and 3 percent a doctoral degree; 6 percent did not possess a four-year college degree
- 76 percent earned less than $100,000 per year and 24 percent earned over $100,000; the median income was $75,000 to $100,000
- 30 percent of the participants identified themselves as single (never married), 53 percent as married, 15 percent as unmarried living with a partner, and 2 percent as divorced, separated, or widowed; one-third of the participants had children; and data were not collected on sexual orientation
- 82 percent self-identified as White, 9 percent Asian or Pacific Islander, 7 percent Black, 5 percent Hispanic, and 1 percent Native American (survey participants could select more than one choice)

Job Search and Employer Selection Criteria

Given our earlier discussion of Millennials' pervasive use of technology tools, it would be reasonable to assume they relied most heavily on such tools to conduct their job search (e.g., using LinkedIn, Vault, and other online job search and networking tools). While it was clear that technology allowed Millennials to research job openings and potential employers, our study found that the most common approach to finding employment included referrals from friends, relatives, and others, with 45 percent of participants stating that they used this approach. This suggests that, despite living in a virtual age, many Millennials continue to make use of more traditional, face-to-face networking techniques for their job search. By contrast, only 15 percent of Millennials stated that they used social media tools such as LinkedIn.

Our study results confirm that the top five qualities that Millennials seek in a potential employer are career growth opportunities, salary, benefits, job security, and work-life balance. "Career growth opportunities" scored highest among the surveyed cohort, which perhaps reflects the fact that most of the individuals surveyed are in the very early stages of their careers. Work-life balance scored the highest (44% of survey participants) among criteria participants rated as "extremely important." We explore this issue in a later section of the report.

The high value placed on job security by the survey participants might strike some as surprising given that many "generational consultants" assert that Millennials lack loyalty and are very willing to leave their present employer if better opportunities elsewhere present themselves. For instance, a recent Gallup report claims that six in ten Millennials are "open to different job opportunities, which is . . . the highest percentage among all generations in the workplace."[35] While it may be true that employees do not necessarily expect long-term job security, it is clear from our research that security is nonetheless highly valued by Millennial employees. This is consistent with other recent research on Millennials' intention to stay with their current organizations.[36]

It is interesting to note that "work that contributes to society" was the lowest rated characteristic in the survey. It was rated as not important or only somewhat important by 39 percent of participants, as compared to 28 percent who rated it as very or extremely important. This casts doubt on the conventional wisdom that Millennials are "the most socially conscious generation since the 1960s," at least with regard to this specific sample. Or it may simply be that because they are at an early career stage, these Millennials did not yet rate this dimension among the most important criteria they seek in an employer.

Job Satisfaction

Study participants indicated that they were performing well, were highly motivated, and felt positively about their current work environment. Participants' responses also suggested that they felt that they worked hard, were respected and supported at work, and planned to stay with their present employers. More than 80 percent agreed or strongly agreed that they were willing to put in a great deal of effort beyond that normally expected in order to help their organization be successful. Slightly more than 85 percent said they felt they were treated with respect in their workplaces, versus only 5 percent who said they did not. These findings may challenge another common assertion made about Millennials—that they are rarely satisfied in their current job situation.

There were, however, some themes of dissatisfaction. More than 20 percent disagreed or strongly disagreed that it was easy to manage their work and personal lives well in their current roles; 15 percent did not believe their employer cared about their well-being; 14 percent were not satisfied with the opportunities they had to learn new skills, and 14 percent did not feel their jobs were meaningful. These factors might support the research that indicates that many Millennials might be inclined to seek out new jobs with relative frequency. In spite of these concerns, more than three-quarters of both men and women agreed or strongly agreed that their managers cared about their opinions and their well-being ("well-being" here was defined broadly to include physical, emotional, and financial wellness). Perhaps, not surprisingly, those who felt most strongly that their managers cared about their well-being were the most satisfied with their jobs. In fact, the differences were quite dramatic. Those who strongly agreed that their manager cared about their well-being rated their job satisfaction 4.2 on a scale of 1 to 5 (5 being the highest level of satisfaction). By contrast, those who strongly disagreed that their manager cared about their well-being scored only 2.2 out of 5 on job satisfaction (fig. 1).

Overall, slightly more than 60 percent of the participants said that they plan to stay in their jobs for some time. However, over one-quarter agreed or strongly agreed (17.2% and 8.8%, respectively) that they often thought about quitting their jobs. When asked, "If you were to voluntarily leave your current employer, how likely is it that each of the following reasons would be the cause?," the participants' main reasons included: to make more money, to move forward in their careers, to pursue work that is more aligned with their passions, and to have more flexibility or achieve a better work-life balance. The men in our study were more likely (76%) than the women (66%) to report they would leave their jobs in order to make more money. The women

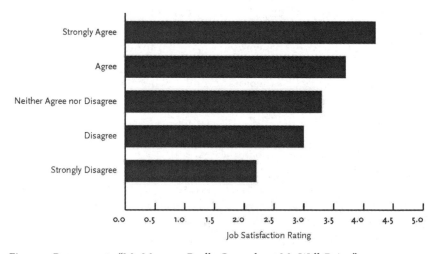

Figure 1. Responses to "My Manager Really Cares about My Well-Being"

were more likely than men to say they would leave to take less stressful jobs (33% to 23%) and to raise their children (31% to 17%).

Career Management

Participants were asked a number of questions to better understand how young adults navigate their careers. The questions explored the importance of career to their sense of identity, what they hoped to achieve in their careers, and whether they were satisfied with their career progression. Forty percent of survey respondents claimed that their career was not central to their identity or how they would define themselves (fig. 2). This figure is striking given that slightly more than 60 percent rated their careers as important or extremely important. Still, the participants consistently distinguished between themselves and their work: slightly more than two-thirds of participants agreed with the statement "work is only a small part of who I am," and nearly three out of five disagreed with the statement that "most of their interests centered on their professions."

Despite prioritizing their personal lives more highly than their professional ones, participants still expressed a strong desire to take on increasingly challenging tasks at work (82%), to be regarded as an expert in a particular area

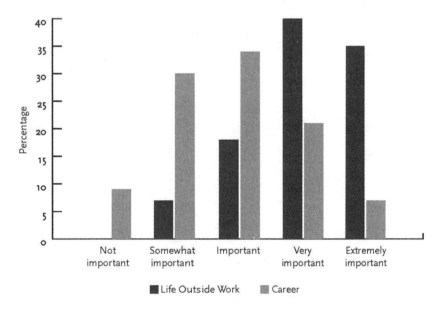

Figure 2. Life vs. Work, Importance to Identity

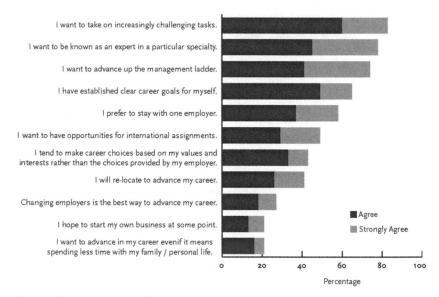

Figure 3. Employee Career Goals

(77%), and to advance professionally (74%). At the same time, however, only 20 percent agreed that they would choose advancement if that meant less time for familial and personal commitments (and only 4% strongly agreed with this statement; fig. 3). The low level of support for this last statement demonstrates again the unwillingness of Millennials at this stage of their career to compromise their personal lives for their work. This was true for participants who were the parents in the study as well as for childless Millennials.

Valued Employer-Provided Resources

In the study, we also explored which employer-provided resources and supports were viewed as most utilized and most valuable in facilitating career growth. Eighty-two percent of study participants reported that "access to informal mentors" was helpful, and 71 percent of participants reported that "ad hoc career advice (at times other than formal performance evaluations)"— was helpful in supporting their development. It is also noteworthy that they found these informal development approaches to be more helpful than "performance evaluation reviews that include development planning," which was the lowest rated form of support provided by their employer although also the most widely used approach across all organizations in the study. While utilization of funding to pursue college courses or a college or graduate degree was used by a smaller number of employees (25% and 27%, respectively), these tuition assistance benefits were the most highly valued, especially those aimed at supporting employees to complete a college or advanced degree.

Defining Career Success

Salary and salary growth rate were considered important indicators of career success, with over 95 percent of participants ranking these as either important, very important, or extremely important). However, job satisfaction ranked even higher than salary measures, at 98 percent. In fact, job satisfaction was rated as very important or extremely important by 84 percent, compared to 76 percent for salary. These findings support a 2008 study of the Silent Generation, Baby Boomers, Generation X, and Generation Y (Millennials) that also found that job satisfaction, followed by salary, were the two highest rated measures of career success for all four generations. In our study, the development of new skills, work achievements, and achievement of personal goals were also important career success measures (about 95%). Finally, work life balance (94%) was viewed as extremely important by 44 percent, which was the highest "extremely important" rating.[37]

It has become almost conventional wisdom that most Millennials are dissatisfied in their careers and rate of advancement. However, nearly 70 percent of the young professionals participating in our study reported that they were satisfied with the success they had achieved in their careers, and three out of five were satisfied with the progress they have made toward their goals for advancement. The lowest level of satisfaction according to participants (51% vs. a range of 56–70% for all other factors; fig. 4) was in meeting their goals for income, which has been mentioned as one of their most important career success measures and the most likely reason they would leave their present employer. Clearly, it is important to focus on and understand this relatively low level of satisfaction. That said, salary is a difficult area in which to satisfy everyone. As Frederick Herzberg points out in his seminal work on motivation, salary is an extrinsic reward, a "hygienic" factor, rather than a "motivating" one (i.e., a poor salary will be demotivating, but at some point, increasing salary does not increase either intrinsic satisfaction or motivation). While it is important to maintain competitive salaries, salary may never score the highest on employee satisfaction surveys and, at a certain level, will have diminishing returns when it comes to increasing employee engagement.

The responses to this portion of the survey thus suggest that it's critical for employers to look at certain factors when considering retention, motivation,

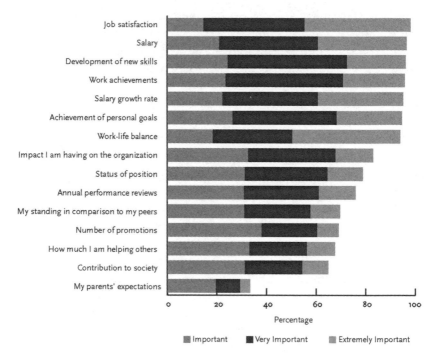

Figure 4. Career Success Measures

and overall satisfaction of Millennial workers. These factors include providing satisfying work about which Millennial employees are passionate and that provide opportunities for development; creating opportunities for them to advance their careers in ways that are consistent with their career-life goals; and finding optimal work-life integration.

Work-Life Balance

Throughout the study, the importance of work-life balance for Millennials was a recurring theme. The majority of the young adults surveyed felt that life outside of work was more important than their careers and this proved to be the case regardless of gender, marital status, or parental status of the respondents. The majority of participants (66%) reported that life outside of work was more important, while only 23 percent said they were of equal importance, and 11 percent responded that their career was more important.

For those who were married or partnered with children, more than 90 percent said that their career decisions are made in terms of how they will affect their families to a considerable or great extent. We also found that study participants who had discussions about career or life goals with their partners at least monthly scored significantly higher on life satisfaction than those who had those conversations only once or twice a year. Participants who had more frequent career or life goal discussions with their partners also reported having greater support from them in their roles as workers. Overall, the large majority of participants felt their spouses or partners supported them as workers and contributed to their careers, although there was a significant difference between men and women—87 percent of men agreed or strongly agreed that their spouses or partners understood the demands of their work, while 78 percent of women agreed or strongly agreed.

Through our research and the research of many others, it is apparent that work-life balance is highly valued by this generation. Looking specifically at the experience of Millennial parents, this value seems to be equally the result of a need for greater balance due to the high number of dual-career couples, as well as a sincere desire on the part of men to be more actively involved in the home and with child rearing. In our study, we found that, while Millennial fathers were somewhat more career-centric than the Millennial mothers were, the differences were not as dramatic as one might expect.

Millennial Fathers

The experience of Millennial dads might best reveal how much things have changed for this group. In our sample, we found that the Millennial dads could be broken into three groups of nearly equal size. The first we called *traditional fathers*. These men stated that they felt their wives should do more than they do on the caregiving front, and that she does. The second group, which we labeled *egalitarian fathers*, felt that caregiving should be divided 50–50, and stated that was indeed the case. The third group felt they should be sharing child care 50–50 but were not (their wives were doing more than they were). We labeled this third group *conflicted fathers*.

This means that two-thirds of Millennial fathers in our workplace study are striving to achieve a more equitable balance between breadwinning and caregiving. Among these men, half, the egalitarian fathers, are achieving this, but the other half, the conflicted fathers are not.

By looking at these three groups, it was also possible to see which of these reported the highest levels of career and life satisfaction. The results were clear, and in some cases, surprising. Across the majority of a wide range of questions about their work and home lives, egalitarian fathers reported the highest levels of satisfaction. Even when it came to finding it easy to balance work and family, the egalitarians scores were the most positive in spite of the fact that they were doing the most on the home front. Traditional fathers scored somewhat lower than the egalitarian fathers, and conflicted dads reported the lowest scores. Those who aspired to share care giving equally with their partners, but did not, were the least satisfied with both their work and home life.

So this research study, along with the research of many other scholars, would suggest that there *are* differences in how work-life balance is prioritized by today's young adults compared with past generations, and there are also some similarities. The priority placed on work-life integration (or balance) may indeed become the key to workplace engagement and the defining criteria for success for today's Millennial workforce.

SUMMARY

The Millennial generation has been saddled with many labels and stereotypes. Often, these labels have been based on less than rigorous research. As Jeffrey Arnett and his colleagues stated in a piece on this topic, "although denigrating the young is an ancient tradition, it has taken on a new vehemence in our time."[38] Clearly, Millennials have been profoundly influenced by a number of societal trends, including the rise in pervasive technologies, changing gender roles, and dramatic changes in the employment contract. These and other meta-trends have led to significant changes in how young people communicate and how they view their careers and their lives. However, is it fair to assume that these changes really suggest a fundamental shift in the attitudes, ambition, and priorities of this talented, educated cohort of young people?

Our research and that of others suggests that while it is important to understand how these trends have impacted the perspectives of young adults, it is also important not to make sweeping generalizations or inferential leaps about the character of this cohort. We have found that Millennials who were more satisfied with their jobs scored higher on work-effort and intention to stay with their employers. They also tended to be happier with their careers and their lives overall. We also found that organizational cultures and managers who actively support their employees tend to have more satisfied young adult workers. Managers, in particular, seem to have considerable impact on Millennials' job satisfaction.

Much has been written about the "fact" that employee loyalty is a "thing of the past" and not a value held by most Millennials. There has also been a widely held belief that this lack of loyalty leads young professionals to see job-hopping as the surest means to career advancement. In our study, however, these points did not hold true. If Millennials lack loyalty, it may be because they feel they need to be cautious in response to the large-scale downsizing that they have observed in their lifetime. In our research, the majority of young adults said that they plan to stay in their jobs for some time, and at a rate of more than two to one, study participants said they believed that staying with their employers was their preferred strategy to advancement versus leaving their organizations.

In recent decades, women have made tremendous strides in their numbers in higher education and their numbers and level in the workplace. These changes have begun to minimize the differences between how young men and women view work and family issues, though some remain. When it comes to thoughts about career advancement, for example, we see that 82 percent of young men would like to advance to a position where they can have a greater influence on policy decisions in the company, compared to 71 percent of young women in our study; and 74 percent of young men have a strong desire to advance to a position in senior management, compared to 67 percent of women. But while the women in our research did report somewhat lower aspirations for top-level jobs than the men, the differences were not parallel to the actual difference in men versus women in most senior management positions, where men greatly outnumber women in most organizations. This is especially true in the senior ranks of large corporations where women, for example, make up less than 5 percent of CEOs in Fortune 1000 companies.[39]

Finally, the importance of "life over work" was evident in our research and that of others. The majority of young adults that we sampled clearly felt that their lives outside of work were much more important to their sense of identity than their careers were. Rather than being work-centric, most of the young professionals we surveyed report being dual-centric, with a strong desire for a meaningful life and an identity based on much more than job titles or organizational status.

Although a very high percentage of respondents wanted to take on increasingly challenging tasks, develop their expertise, and advance up the career ladder, few were willing to pursue these goals at the expense of their personal lives and time with their families. This finding is hardly unique to our sample. Most studies have found that individuals derive much more meaning and satisfaction from important relationships and their families than they do from their careers. This was clearly supported in our study and explains why work-life integration is so important to these Millennials.

Notes

1. William Strauss and Neil Howe, *Millennials Rising: The Next Great Generation* (New York: Vintage, 2000).

2. Eric Hoover, "The Millennial Muddle," Students, *Chronicle of Higher Education*, October 11, 2009, accessed October 14, 2016, at https://chronicle.com.

3. Charles Arthur, "The History of Smartphones: A Timeline," Tech, *Guardian*, January 24, 2012, accessed June 14, 2016, at www.theguardian.com.

4. Monica Anderson, "The Demographics of Device Ownership," Internet, Science and Tech, Pew Research Center, October 29, 2015.

5. *The Millennial Generation Research Review*, National Chamber Foundation, 2012.

6. Sherry Turkle, *Reclaiming Conversation: The Power of Talk in a Digital Age* (New York: Penguin Press, 2015).

7. Jennifer J. Deal, David G. Altman, and Steven G. Roselberg, "Millennials at Work: What We Know and What We Need to Do (If Anything)," *Journal of Business and Psychology* 25, no. 2 (2010): 191–99, doi:10.2007/s10869-010-9177-2.

8. Anderson, *Demographics of Device Ownership*.

9. *Millennial Generation Research Review*.

10. Matt Rocheleau, "Student Loan Debt Has Tripled to $1.23 Trillion—Yes, Trillion," *Boston Globe*, May 18, 2016, accessed June 5, 2016, at www.bostonglobe.com.

11. Samantha Raphelson, "Amid the Stereotypes, Some Facts about Millennials," New Boom series, *NPR*, November 18, 2014, accessed June 2, 2016, at www.npr.org. Jeffrey Sparshott, "Congratulations, Class of 2015: You're the Most Indebted Ever (for Now)," Real Time Economics, *Wall Street Journal*, May 8, 2015, accessed June 13, 2016, at http://blogs.wsj.com/.

12. *Millennial Generation Research Review*.

13. Tamar Lewin, "Most College Students Don't Earn a Degree in 4 Years, Study Finds," *New York Times*, December 2, 2012, accessed June 14, 2016, at www.nytimes.com.

14. Raphelson, "Amid the Stereotypes."

15. *The Rising Cost of Not Going to College*, Social and Demographic Trends, Pew Research Center, February 11, 2014.

16. "Table 318.30. Bachelor's, Master's, and Doctor's Degrees Conferred by Post-secondary Institutions, by Sex of Student and Discipline Division: 2013–14," National Center for Education Statistics, 2016, accessed April 20, 2016, at www.nces.ed.gov.

17. Eileen Pateen and Kim Parker, "A Gender Reversal on Career Aspirations: Young Women Now Top Young Men in Valuing a High-Paying Career," Social and Demographic Trends, Pew Research Center, April 19, 2012.

18. Ibid.

19. "Statistical Overview of Women in the Workforce," Quick Take, Knowledge Center, Catalyst, April 6, 2016.

20. Wendy Wang, Kim Parker, and Paul Taylor, *Breadwinner Moms—Mothers Are the Sole or Primary Provider in Four-in-Ten Households with Children; Public Conflicted about the Growing Trend*, Social Trends, Pew Research Center, May 29, 2013.

21. EY [Ernst & Young Global], "Global Generations: A Global Study of Work-Life Challenges Across Generations," 2015, accessed June 30, 2016, at www.ey.com/.

22. Kathleen Gerson, *The Unfinished Revolution: How a New Generation Is Reshaping Family, Work, and Gender in America* (New York: Oxford University Press, 2010).

23. Pateen and Parker, "Gender Reversal."

24. Morley Winograd and Michael D. Hais, "Race? No, Millennials Care Most about Gender Equality," *Atlantic*, October 25, 2013, accessed June 2, 2016, at www.theatlantic.com.

25. Louis Uchitelle, *The Disposable American: Layoffs and Their Consequences* (New York: Alfred A. Knopf, 2006).

26. Elizabeth Warren and Amelia Warren Tyagi, *The Two-Income Trap: Why Middle-Class Parents Are Going Broke* (New York: Basic Books, 2004).

27. Cathleen Benko and Anne Weisberg, *Mass Career Customization: Aligning the Workplace with Today's Nontraditional Workforce* (Cambridge, MA: Harvard Business Review Press, 2007); Brad Harrington and Douglas T. Hall, *Career Management and Work-Life Integration: Using Self-Assessment to Navigate Contemporary Careers* (Thousand Oaks, CA: Sage Publications, 2007).

28. Benko and Weisberg, *Mass Career Customization*; Harrington and Hall, *Career Management and Work-Life Integration*.

29. Ben Casselman, "Enough Already about the Job-Hopping Millennials," Economics, *FiveThirtyEight*, May 5, 2015, accessed August 4, 2016, at http://fivethirtyeight.com.

30. Jeanne Meister, "The Future of Work: Job Hopping Is the 'New Normal' for Millennials," Leadership, *Forbes*, August 14, 2012, accessed August 4, 2016, at www.forbes.com.

31. Jean Sahady, "Dell Computers *Really* Wants You to Wants You to Work from Home . . . If You Want To," Reinventing Work, Money, CNN.com, June 9, 2016, accessed April 18, 2017, at http://money.cnn.com.

32. Steve Matthews and Victoria Stilwell, "American on the Move Becomes Stay-Home Nation for Young: Economy," *Bloomberg*, May 12, 2014, accessed August 3, 2016, at www.bloomberg.com.

33. Joseph Berger, "Suburbs Try to Prevent an Exodus as Young Adults Move to Cities and Stay," N.Y. Region, *New York Times*, April 17, 2014, accessed April 18, 2017, at www.nytimes.com.

34. Kathleen Elkins, "The 10 Best Big Cities for Educated Millennials," Careers, *Business Insider*, May 12, 2015, accessed August 3, 2016, at www.businessinsider.com/.

35. Brandon Rigoni and Amy Adkins, "What Millennials Want from a New Job," *Harvard Business Review*, May 11, 2016, accessed June 18, 2016, at https://hbr.org.

36. Jennifer Deal and Alec Levenson, "Millennials Play the Long Game," *Strategy + Business*, October 5, 2015.

37. Nicky Dries, Roland Pepermans, and Evelien De Kerpel, "Exploring Four Generations' Beliefs about Career," *Journal of Managerial Psychology* 23, no. 8 (2008): 907–28.

38. Jeffrey Arnett, Kali Trzesniewski, and Brent Donnellan, "The Dangers of Generational Myth-Making: Rejoinder to Twenge," *Emerging Adulthood* 1, no. 1 (2013): 17–20.

39. "Women in the Workplace 2015," LeanIn.Org and McKinsey & Co., 2015, accessed April 18, 2017, at http://womenintheworkplace.com.

Bibliography

Harrington, Brad, Fred Van Deusen, Jennifer Fraone, and Jeremiah Morelock. *How Millennials Navigate Their Careers: Research Report*. Boston College Center for Work and Family, 2015.

Mobile Technology Fact Sheet. Pew Research Center, December 27, 2013.

Wang, Wendy, and Kim Parker. *Record Share of Americans Have Never Married*. Pew Research Center, September 24, 2014.

Wang, Wendy, and Paul Taylor. *Millennials' Attitudes about Marriage*. Pew Research Center, March 9, 2011.

PART THREE

SYNTHESIS

9 to 5 to 0 and 1

The Future of Work

RUDY FAUST

Director of the Urban Forum Michael Pagano opened the 2016 Urban Forum with a collection of seemingly positive benchmark statistics. Unemployment was at a low point, both in Illinois and in the United States, and other indicators seemed to point to an altogether improving employment picture. These numbers mask the structural issues—migration, training, and education—that both the white papers and panels address.

The three panels were formally titled "Evolving Pathways to Work," "The Jobless Economy," and "Bridges of Walls? Immigration and Trade Policy," but the conversations ranged as widely as did the panelists' backgrounds, from community activists and academics to entrepreneurs, industrialists, and even a Nobel Laureate. While the organizers of the Urban Forum charged only the first panel with explicitly addressing education, it seemed that the entire convening was shot through with concerns about how both the public and private sectors might educate and train both those in the current workforce who might be most affected by technological and demographic trends and also more generally the rising generations.

EVOLVING PATHWAYS TO WORK

The promise of a decent job after gaining a secondary education evaporated long ago. Now, even a college education is no longer a guarantee of employment. The speakers on the first panel tackled the even broader issues of both educating and training the rising generation and offering the necessary skills for the current workforce, so they are not left behind by the change.

Moderator John McCarron, a former *Chicago Tribune* urban affairs writer, opened with three daunting challenges. First, he cited the worsening gap between youths and young adults from communities of color and their peers, as highlighted in "Lost: The Crisis of Jobless and Out of School Teens and Young Adults in Chicago, Illinois, and the U.S.," a study released a few months earlier by the Great Cities Institute at the University of Illinois at Chicago.[1] Second, he mentioned that although the number of manufacturing jobs in the United States have been rising over the past few years, the employers have had trouble filling the positions. Finally, while college students still earn more money than those with less educational attainment, the ever-rising cost of educational debt incurred by students, as discussed in Brad Harrington's white paper, threatens insolvency.

The first speaker, Theresa Mintle, is currently the president and CEO of the Chicagoland Chamber of Commerce, but her previous positions include chief-of-staff appointments at both the mayor of Chicago's office and the Chicago Transportation Authority. She opened the panel discussion with an immediate salvo against the current drive from the highest level of government that everyone should attain a college degree. The move has come at the cost of vocational training at the high-school level. Furthermore, community colleges are now often geared toward transitioning their students to a four-year college. While there is certainly merit to the both impulses—one would find it difficult to argue against either strengthening math and reading skills or easing the transition financially and academically into college—local businesses found that they were short of new skilled workers. The City of Chicago, starting under Mayor Richard M. Daley and accelerated by his successor, Rahm Emmanuel, has responded by most notably specializing the city college campuses to concentrate related skills into single campuses, such as STEM (science, technology, engineering, and math), hospitality, and so on. Although she was part of the mayors' efforts, Mintle argued that it was the business partnerships that hold the most potential for bridging the gaps mentioned by McCarron. Members of the Chamber of Commerce have initiated internship programs that employ high-school students. The program not only teaches general workplace skills but also specific skills in the students' areas of interest. The ultimate hope is that a technology student, for instance, might gain both immediately applicable job skills and applied knowledge that helps bring alive college-level subjects.

Juan Salgado, president and CEO of the Instituto del Progreso Latino and MacArthur Fellow (also known as the "genius grant") class of 2015, made the case that that "community groups [such as his institute] are leaders in the evolution"—the evolving pathway to the workforce—pointing out that the Instituto del Progreso Latino initiated a health sciences charter high school before the city's charter system was in place. Additionally, while the high-school and community-college systems are seeing reforms, there are many outside the system, especially immigrants and other adult learners, who require different approaches. The institute focuses on those among the 36 million adults in the Chicago area who read below a tenth-grade level. One way they do this is through its four-hundred-student elementary school attended by adult learners, largely speakers of English as a second language. This holistic approach works on the assumption that creating an environment where the parents as well children are in school will raise the educational attainment and income of both groups.

The conversation remained focused on the important place of the family in employment outcomes, as James Heckman concluded the formal presentations. The University of Chicago professor, founding faculty of the Harris School of Public Policy, and Nobel laureate for Economics focused on the so-called soft skills—cooperation, self-control, perseverance, and other social skills—that researchers have found lead to success later in life. The common misperception on a policy level is that there is no means to measure these skills, which Heckman immediately challenged. Unfortunately, according to Heckman, the current consequence is that "we have somehow educated ourselves out of common sense knowledge." While formal education remains important for attainment of skills, the odds of success are largely dependent on more quotidian factors. For instance, researchers know with a high degree of probability children's college readiness based on their family state and the children's behavior at age five.

He presented Abraham Lincoln as a brief case study. Our sixteenth president became a lawyer through the then-common means of apprenticeship, without any formal schooling in the field. The partnerships and development that happens outside of the classroom often has a powerful effect on the success of any student.

While James Heckman continued to focus on the family's place in educational and career opportunity, he acknowledged the sometimes-troubled and paternalistic history of the discussion. Rather than a judgmental and intrusive policy, Heckman argued for reinforcing programs that promote strong family structures. For instance, child-care subsidies are more effective than regressive penalties. His preferred method is to incentivize employers. As the presentations moved to a discussion with the panel, he elaborated that he prefers tax incentives and a certain degree of deregulation to promote U.S. competitiveness, noting in the spirit of the future-looking nature of the panel that the nation faces a much more competitive world than it did during its presumptive hegemony in the post–World War II era.

The conversation continued with Mintle supporting less regulation on businesses, and specifically, opposing the push for raising the minimum wage and family-leave initiatives then underway in Chicago. She argued that the measures, if not implemented on state or federal levels, would distort the pathways to work by driving entry-level jobs across state lines.

Salgado countered that working families are already juggling multiple low-paying jobs, so they might actually desire fewer, higher-paying jobs. Most of the families he serves are living on an income of $19,000 per year.

Ultimately, the discussion concluded on policies that might both promote private business activity and offer pathways to better pay, without penalties.

THE JOBLESS ECONOMY

The remarkable technological advances of recent years reach into every vocation with efficiencies that come at the cost of existing jobs. The acceleration of these technologies means that the so-called jobless future might be closer than previously thought.

Sarah Karp, the education reporter for Chicago radio station WBEZ, moderated a panel of thinkers with a wealth of educational experience, who are charged with developing those who will, in turn, lead in the future. The panel consisted of George Crabtree, director of the Joint Center for Energy Storage (JCES) at Argonne National Laboratory, and UIC professor of physics; Julie Friedman Steele, founder and CEO of the 3D Printer Experience and chair of the board of directors and interim executive director of the World Future Society; and Beth Swanson, who is vice president of Strategy and Programs for the Joyce Foundation, and who has previously held education administration positions.

Crabtree looked to the economic epochs since the industrial revolution to gain perspective on the waves of labor. The first revolution was the mechanization of labor, which resulted in the centralization of labor into factories and a radical increase in production. It of course brought with it attendant cultural shifts and immediate displacement, but the culture was able to adapt with it.

The second, and current, wave, which he calls "machine learning," has the microprocessor computer at its center. In this current revolution human intelligence and the resulting activities are superseded by computer control. As examples, he referred to the victories of IBM's Deep Blue computer over the world's top chess grandmasters; the accelerating self-driving car capabilities that can (when fully networked) drive without incident; and in his own advanced energy storage laboratory, complete tests that can now be simulated on powerful computers. While the current technologies are already displacing jobs and doing so farther along the scale of skilled labor than ever before, Crabtree observed that the rate of change is accelerating. He is loathe to predict the ultimate consequences of the changes, but he notes the possibility of a jobless future if we cede economic decisions to machines. But Crabtree emphasized that humanity would adapt. He pointed to the Millennial Generation's desire for hyper-personalization in online experiences and beyond. The ultra-personal economy would indeed mark a cultural shift, but would spark a new economy . . . and new jobs.

As the chair of the World Future Society and the founder of an educational nonprofit literally on the street, Julie Friedman Steele was charged with speaking broadly to how to face the jobless future. Her approach aligned with Crabtree's assertion that the so-called jobless future will not take the presumed form. So what is to be done? Friedman Steele first outlined the traits that the World Future Society has identified as necessary for promoting readiness for the accelerating change on the horizon. Some of the traits—willingness to be a lifelong learner, empathy, and cooperation—spoke directly to and continued James Heckman's conversation about soft skills. To this conversation, Friedman Steele added that one must also become a "lifelong unlearner" and imagine alternate futures, or alternate realities. This epistemic flexibility goes against human nature, but is necessary for the current pace of changes. She used the example of Sir Ken Robinson's TED Talk, *Changing Education Paradigms*, and asserted that too often education kills creativity.[2]

While her work at the World Future Society is largely speculative and theoretical, Friedman Steele's work as the founder of the 3-D Printer Experience has illuminated some of the work necessary in implementing these goals. The technology in question, often called additive manufacturing, is part of the massive change in the workforce. Yet, she observed, the "Gartner Hype Cycle," in which a wave of excitement and overinflated expectation for a new technology is followed by a "trough of despair" is in effect for many advances.[3] There is a certain amount of stagnation, of both adoption and vision, that Friedman Steele believes needs to be shaken loose. Her goal is to shorten the trough of despair from the standard few years of stagnation within one session.

While Friedman Steele focused on the soft skills, Beth Swanson returned the discussion to education with a discussion that synthesized parts of the previous panelists' assertions. Her concern was an immediate future that might have either low- or high-paying jobs, but nothing in the middle.

To alleviate her concern, the Joyce Foundation, like the Instituto del Progresso Latino and the Chamber of Commerce, invests in apprenticeships to build the skills and connections to industries—in the case of Joyce, financial—that have the resources to move forward. Likewise, she asserted that education needs brighter lines to college and work. In the discussion, she noted that classrooms, unlike the workplace, look much as they did seventy-five years ago.

Moderator Sarah Karp brought up other cities that might face a secular decline. In particular, she mentioned Youngstown, Ohio, the subject of a 2015 *Atlantic* article titled "A World without Work," and asked if we will see deep valleys between jobs and joblessness.[4] Crabtree and Friedman urged the audience to look beyond our current valuation of jobs as the ultimate definition of a productive life.

BRIDGES OR WALLS? IMMIGRATION AND TRADE POLICY

As recently as the 2012 election cycle, immigration and trade policy appeared headed toward consensus within national politics, yet the 2016 Urban Forum was held during a national, and presidential, election campaign in which assumptions were attacked from both ends of the political spectrum.

The final panel, moderated by Chip Mitchel of WBEZ, represented a wide range of viewpoints. Oscar Chacón, cofounder and executive director of Alianza Americas, gave voice both to his experience as an immigrant to the United States from war-torn El Salvador in 1980, and to his work as an advocate for other immigrants. Héctor Cordero-Guzmán, a professor of urban and public affairs at Baruch College, directly challenged many of the more facile assumptions about how capitalism and trade benefit mobility. Finally, Pin Ni, founder and CEO of Wanxiang America, brought the perspective of an immigrant and entrepreneur.

Cordero-Guzmán noted that the largest employers in the world are ManpowerGroup and Walmart. The trend that he sees is a consolidation of wealth, with an increasing gap between the very wealth and poor, regardless of borders. He criticized the suppression of wages that comes as a result of cheaper goods but argued that the most effective way of countering the larger trends is at the community level, with organizations such as the Instituto del Progreso Latino and Alianza Americas.

The conversation continued to focus on the borderless economy, but now from the perspective of a businessperson and immigrant who is directly affected by policy in both his personal and professional life. Pin Ni related his story. He originally immigrated to the United States to pursue a doctorate at the University of Kentucky. In twenty years, he built Wanxiang America from a small trading house for his father-in-law's auto parts company in China to a large U.S.-based parts manufacturer. He asserted that people everywhere are looking for a better deal as well as a better product, so market forces will forever strain against borders. He first opened with an example to set a benchmark. When he was a student, a telephone call to China cost four dollars per minute—more than his hourly salary at the time. He praised the improvements in connectivity, on all fronts, since then. Although challenges remain, he remains optimistic that the trend towards more open trade will benefit both countries.

An example of the new ways was A123 Battery, which came out of MIT research and received federal funding in 2010. By 2012 it was hemorrhaging cash and was for sale. Wanxiang America, even though it was Chinese-owned, purchased the company and within eighteen months returned it to profitability, thus saving U.S. jobs.[5] While the deal was not without its difficulties, it is now exporting 80 percent of its product. The World Future Society member might here stress the importance of unlearning and imagining multiple futures, as a project meant as a U.S. tool for recovery from recession became a multinational project. Globalization is a reality, and Pin Ni's example shows, if anything, that there are no simplistic answers to what may be a simplistically defined issue.

Oscar Chacón brought another immigrant perspective, specifically a social-justice perspective. Since his immigration from El Salvador in 1980, he has worked for immigrant rights in the United States. He agreed that capital and ideas indeed move across borders with greater ease than ever before, yet the movement of people is becoming more difficult. He argued for universal health and employment benefits across international borders, so mobility becomes a choice made out of free will, rather out of desperation or dissatisfaction. The conversation continued regarding immigration with Cordero-Guzmán building on the concept of mobility for return. The consequence of erecting barriers has meant that, instead of allowing workers to move temporarily between the United States and their home countries for employment, they are forced to bring their families here for a long period or to migrate permanently. Both Cordero-Guzmán and Chacón made the point that open borders would not mean a flood of migration, as many people prefer to remain in their home country.

Pin Ni remarked that, as difficult as it is to control the movement of people, controlling capital is even more difficult. He used two examples as illustration. He criticized the restoration of tariffs for steel, noting how the cost then is pushed down the line to the manufacturers who work the raw material, raising their prices, and making them less competitive on the global market. Likewise, the automation mentioned by George Crabtree knows no bounds. Pin Ni pointed out that the cost of labor in China has reached a point that robots are replacing two thousand factory jobs a year in China. He stressed that there are definite downsides to progress, but any move backward would further push automation, freer trade, and so on elsewhere—capital is looking for the path of least resistance.

Cordero-Guzmán and Oscar Chacón argued the necessity of raising the salary floor for every worker to counter the downward pressure, worldwide. Chacón repeated that the rising wealth has been inequitably distributed. Codero-Guzmán concluded on a hopeful note with the observation that globalization has also raised the amount of awareness of and exposure that people have to one another. These interactions will ultimately result in progress.

The 2016 Urban Forum concluded seven weeks before the November 8 election, and the room was generally optimistic. Although seismic changes are upon us now, the discussions regarding the primacy of education, forward-thinking hope, and understanding across borders are perhaps even more relevant as we move forward.

Notes

1. Teresa L. Cordova and Matthew D. Wilson, "Lost: The Crisis of Jobless and Out of School Teens and Young Adults in Chicago, Illinois and the U.S.," produced for Alternative Schools Network, Great Cities Institute, University of Illinois at Chicago. February 1, 2016, accessed March 28, 2017, at https://greatcities.uic.edu.

2. Ken Robinson, "Changing Education Paradigms," filmed October 2010, TED video, 11:40, accessed April 20, 2017, at https://www.ted.com.

3. "Gartner Hype Cycle," Research Methodologies, Gartner, accessed April 20, 2017, at www.gartner.com.

4. Derek Thompson, "A World without Work," *Atlantic*, July/August 2015, accessed April 20, 2017, at www.theatlantic.com/.

5. Susan Berfield, "Batteries with a Political Charge," Businessweek, *Bloomberg*, October 29, 2015, accessed April 20, 2017, at www.bloomberg.com.

Contributors

XÓCHITL BADA is associate professor of Latin American and Latino studies at the University of Illinois at Chicago. She earned her doctorate in sociology from the University of Notre Dame. Her research interests include immigrant access to political and social rights, Black-Latino relations, immigrant organizing strategies, rural development in labor expulsion regions, and transnational labor advocacy mobilization in Mexico and the United States. She is a co-convener of *De aquí y de allá. Jóvenes sin fronteras*, the First Strategic Dialogue between Latino DACAmented leaders and young deported leaders celebrated in Mexico City in 2015. Her recent research has appeared in the journals *Population, Space, and Place*; *Practicing Anthropology*; *Revista de la Asociación Latinoamericana de Sociología Rural*; *Migraciones Internacionales*; *Latino Studies*; and the *Latinamericanist*. Her book, *Mexican Hometown Associations in Chicagoacán: From Local to Transnational Civic Engagement* (2014) demonstrates how and why emergent forms of citizen participation practiced by Mexican Hometown Associations (HTAs) engage simultaneously with political elites in Mexico and the United States, and the ways they operate at multiple scales, from the local, to the state, national, and international. She is coeditor of *Context Matters: Latino Immigrant Civic Engagement in Nine U.S. Cities*, (bilingual edition, 2010) published by the Woodrow Wilson International Center for Scholars. She is currently analyzing the challenges Mexican citizens face in getting access to birth certificates in Mexico's rural areas and in consulates across the United States. She is also engaged in two collaborative projects. With Jonathan Fox (American University), she is exploring continuities and changes in rural migration patterns in Mexico's countryside between 2000 and 2010 to inform potential initiatives in favor of the right not to migrate. With Shannon Gleeson, she is researching the role of the Mexican Consulate in protecting the rights of Mexican workers in the United States.

JOHN BRAGELMAN is a doctoral student at University of Illinois at Chicago and a professor at Harold Washington College. His research interests include remedial mathematics education, mathematics identity, and teaching mathematics for social justice in the context of community colleges, particularly with adult learners.

LAURA DRESSER, MSW, PhD, is associate director of the Center on Wisconsin Strategy at the University of Wisconsin–Madison. A labor economist and expert on low-wage work and workforce development systems, she has both written about ways to build stronger labor market systems and worked extensively with labor, business, and community leaders in building them. Dresser has written about low-wage jobs, care work, inequality and labor market reform. A co-editor of *The Gloves-Off Economy: Workplace Standards at the Bottom of America's Labor Market* (2008), she is currently working on the connections between quality care, quality jobs, and minimum wages.

RUDY FAUST is a master's degree candidate in the College of Urban Planning and Public Affairs at the University of Illinois at Chicago.

BETH GUTELIUS, PhD, has done research focusing on low-wage labor markets and global supply chains. She was most recently research associate at the John D. and Catherine T. MacArthur Foundation, where she undertook research on pressing contemporary issues, including the changing nature of work and employment. A founding advisory board member of the Labor Research and Action Network, Gutelius now works with advocates, philanthropists, and scholars to develop original research projects and to analyze emerging trends in order to inform efforts to strengthen workers' rights.

BRAD HARRINGTON is executive director of the Boston College Center for Work & Family (CWF) and a research professor in the Carroll School of Management. His research and teaching focus on career management and work-life integration, the changing role of fathers, and contemporary workforce management strategies. He is the lead author of *Career Management* *and Work-Life Integration* (2007) and *The New Dad*, a seven-year research series exploring the changing role of fathers in the workplace and at home. His most recent study, "How Millennials Navigate Their Careers" (coauthored, 2015), was conducted with 1,100 young adults working in one of five Fortune 500 organizations.

Prior to his arrival at Boston College in 2000, Harrington was an executive with Hewlett-Packard Company for twenty years, serving in global business leadership roles in the United States and Europe.

Harrington is a graduate of Stonehill College and holds advanced degrees in psychology and human resource development from Boston College and Boston University.

GREGORY V. LARNELL, PhD, is a faculty member in the Department of Curriculum and Instruction at the University of Illinois at Chicago. Larnell studies and teaches courses on education and mathematics education with specialized attention to curriculum, learning, identity, and inequity. Some current research projects include studies of postsecondary remediation at two- and four-year colleges, a multi-investigator study of middle-school mathematics teaching professional development and student learning, and a multi-investigator study of elementary teacher education. Larnell's work has been published in the *Journal of Education*, the *Journal for Research in Mathematics Education*, and the *Handbook of Urban Education* among other print outlets, other media, and national and international conference proceedings.

TWYLA T. BLACKMOND LARNELL, PhD, is an assistant professor of political science at Loyola University Chicago. Her research and teaching interests center on urban and local politics and policy. She focuses specifically on the politics of local economic development policy and its implications for racial and ethnic disparities.

NIK THEODORE is a professor in the University of Illinois at Chicago's Department of Urban Planning and Policy. His work focuses on economic restructuring, labor standards, and worker organizing. His research has been published in economics, public policy, and urban studies journals, including the *Cambridge Journal of Economics, International Journal of Urban and Regional Research, Urban Geography, European Urban and Regional Studies, Economic Development Quarterly, Political Geography*. His research on employment issues has been featured in the *New York Times, Wall Street Journal, Time, Chicago Tribune, Los Angeles Times, Washington Post*, CNN,

BBC, *PBS NewsHour*, *All Things Considered* (NPR), *MarketPlace* (NPR), and other media. Prior to joining UIC, he was an Atlantic Fellow in Public Policy at the University of Manchester (England). He is also an editor of *Antipode: A Radical Journal of Geography*.

THE URBAN AGENDA

The University of Illinois Press
is a founding member of the
Association of American University Presses.

———————————————————————

University of Illinois Press
1325 South Oak Street
Champaign, IL 61820-6903
www.press.uillinois.edu